Crisis in the Church

Crisis in the Church

The Plight of Theological Education

JOHN H. LEITH

Westminster John Knox Press
Louisville, Kentucky

Scripture quotations from the New Revised Standard Version
of the Bible are copyright ©1989 by the Division of Christian Education
of the National Council of the Churches of Christ in the U.S.A.
and are used by permission.

Chapter 5, "On Choosing a Seminary Professor" appeared originally
in *The Presbyterian Outlook* (February 27, 1995) and is reprinted,
with adaptations, by permission of *The Presbyterian Outlook,*
Richmond, Virginia.

Book design by Jennifer K. Cox
Cover design by Alec Bartsch
Cover photograph courtesy of Picture Network International Ltd.

First edition
Published by Westminster John Knox Press
Louisville, Kentucky

This book is printed on acid-free paper that meets the
American National Standards Institute Z39.48 standard. ♾

PRINTED IN THE UNITED STATES OF AMERICA
97 98 99 00 01 02 03 04 05 06 — 10 9 8 7 6 5 4 3 2 1

Library of Congress Cataloging-in-Publication Data

Leith, John H.
    Crisis in the church : the plight of theological education / John
H. Leith. — 1st ed.
        p.   cm.
    Includes bibliographical references.
    ISBN 0-664-25700-3 (alk. paper)
    1. Presbyterian Church (U.S.A.)—Clergy—Training of.
    2. Theology—Study and teaching—United States.   I. Title.
BX8969.6.L45 1997
230'.07'35137—dc21   97-12816

Gratefully dedicated to the memory
of two great teachers who became my friends:

ALBERT C. OUTLER

AND

ROLAND H. BAINTON

Contents

Preface

No one is either wise enough or good enough to write about the crisis in theological education. Hence there was some presumption in saying yes to the request of Westminster John Knox Press to write this book, especially after having retired from such tasks. Yet the same strictures may be placed on preaching and teaching theology. As church people, as well as teachers and preachers, we live by justification by grace through faith.

My only qualification is that my whole life has been given to preaching and teaching. I was born in a Presbyterian home and in the fellowship of a Presbyterian church. I can no more leave the Presbyterian Church than I can change my name or leave my family.

I have spent my life either preaching or teaching. I supplied for over two years the Silver Creek Presbyterian Church in Lindale, Georgia, an unincorporated textile mill town, when I was a student at Columbia Theological Seminary, Decatur, Georgia. I would not recommend such a responsibility for any seminary student, but it was an important part of my education, however unwise it may have been as a general practice.

My first work after seminary was gathering a congregation for a preaching service in Spring Hill, Alabama, that became the Spring Hill Presbyterian Church, now the strongest Presbyterian church in that area. I was for three years pastor of the Second Presbyterian Church of Nashville, Tennessee, a suburban congregation, and for eleven years I was pastor of the First Presbyterian Church in Auburn, Alabama, a college town. If I were to choose eleven years to relive, it would probably be the eleven years I was in Auburn. For thirty-one years I taught theology at Union Theological Seminary in Virginia (in Richmond).

I have divided my time after retirement in 1990 between the Center of Theological Inquiry in Princeton, New Jersey, and work on church staffs, in particular Peachtree Presbyterian Church, Atlanta, Georgia; First Presbyterian Church, Charlotte, North Carolina; First Presbyterian Church, Gastonia, North Carolina; White Memorial Presbyterian Church, Raleigh, North Carolina; and First Presbyterian Church, Wilmington, North Carolina. I have always been engaged in presbytery, synod, and General Assembly activities until my retirement, and I served on four General Assembly ad interim committees having to do with polity, creeds, and theology. It is out of these experiences that I write this book.

My ministry has spanned radical changes in the theological commitments of the Presbyterian Church. From 1940 until 1959 I was in conflict with the theological right wing of the church, a theological controversy that was complicated by the racial crisis. In 1958 Columbia Theological Seminary, under pressure from the theological right, rescinded an invitation to me to teach, a decision that was also complicated by the racial conflict. After accepting an invitation to teach at Union Theological Seminary in Virginia, I was in a theological context in which there were no fideistic fundamentalists. Many of the theological right wing left the Presbyterian Church U.S. in the formation of the Presbyterian Church in America in 1973. Yet it has always amazed me how rapidly theological convictions changed in the Presbyterian Church U.S. in the brief period from 1965 to 1975. Perhaps theological positions unfortunately are often more political positions than deeply held convictions.

In recent years I have found myself increasingly in conflict with the left wing. I have also become convinced that the left wing is a greater menace to the health of the Christian community than the right wing was prior to 1960. Certainly the left wing is more, not less, ruthless in imposing its will on the church.

I emphasize in this book the overwhelming priority and significance in the life of the church of what God does and says, not what human beings do and say. Hence it may be important to note that I have been active in community affairs such as civic clubs. I was for about thirty years a member of the Richmond City Committee of the Democratic Party, and I served for twelve years on the Governor's Commission on Seasonal and Migrant Labor in Virginia under appointment by three governors.

The emphasis of this book is on setting the priorities of theological seminaries whose primary task is educating pastors who are to be effective in the work of the ministry. The work of scholars, of research, and of creative theological writers such as Karl Barth or Reinhold Niebuhr are crucial for the church, but this is not the first task of a seminary. In addition there are not many real scholars and there are fewer creative theologians. Even in the case of scholars, they must accomplish the more modest task of interpreting the tradition before they can go beyond it.

I do not claim that my vision is the only vision or that it should stand alone in understanding the crisis we face. We need other commentary on the crisis and challenge. I do claim that my vision of theological education is documentably supported by the work of ministers who share it and who are today in small, medium, or large churches carrying on *effective* work as pastors and congregational leaders.

My observations on seminary education reflect my own experience as a member of the faculty of Union Theological Seminary in Virginia and my own experience as a minister in the Presbyterian Church (U.S.A.) and, earlier, the Presbyterian Church U.S. It is hoped that they will be helpful for theological seminaries generally and for the whole church.

The focus of this book is a critique of trends in theological education that undermine the preparation of men and women for the ministry and for leadership in the congregation and the denomination. My positive convictions about the work of the minister have been stated in other books. In *Introduction to the Reformed Tradition* I described what I believe is the ethos or manner of life of Presbyterianism and Reformed Christians. In *The Reformed Imperative* and *Basic Christian Doctrine* I sought to interpret the Reformed theological tradition on this side of the Enlightenment and the nineteenth century in language and concepts that are intelligible and persuasive to modern people.

My own theological commitments intend to be critically orthodox, that is, to interpret the ancient creeds and Reformed confessions and the works of the great theologians who shaped the Reformed tradition with the clear awareness that the Enlightenment and nineteenth century happened and must be taken seriously. My intention has been to be a competent interpreter and teacher of the tradition, writing theology so the nontheologian can understand, and to be a preacher of the gospel of Jesus Christ persuading people to acknowledge him as Lord and Savior.

I do not believe our only options are dead churches or churches with pop theology and pop culture. Presbyterian churches, authentic in Presbyterian ethos and theology and without equivocation Christian, show great signs of vitality. Young people coming back to the church with their children have given me great hope in every church in which I have worked in the last five years.

The urgency of the theme of this volume is documented in an article in the *Atlantic Monthly* (December 1996) by Charlotte Allen, "The Search for a No-Frills Jesus." Burton Mack has devoted his energies to constructing "Q," a collection of sayings of Jesus which may or may not have existed. According to Mack no one knows how Jesus died. The reconstruction of Q, he believes, will also radically reconstruct the origins of the Christian church. Mack is quoted as saying, "We have had enough apocalypses. We've had enough martyrs. Christianity has had a two-thousand year run, and it's over." The writer also quotes James Robinson as concluding, "I think that Jesus was an important person, one of the most important people who ever lived."

Honorable people can conclude that Jesus was not a Christian and that Christianity is over or they may conclude that Jesus was only an important human being. It is difficult to understand how professors or church leaders who do not believe in the authenticity of the Christ of the Gospels can feel comfortable making their living from the contributions of church people who do. It is even more difficult to understand why church people, in particular institutions and church bureaucrats, wish to sponsor with believers' money those who are seeking to undermine the Christian church and faith.

My debt to many others is very great and cannot be enumerated here in detail. In this book I should say I owe much to ministers who were in charge of youth work when I was in high school, such as Roswell Long of the First Presbyterian Church, Greenwood, South Carolina, and F. B. Mayes, who directed the synod's young people's conferences. I obviously owe much to my seminary teachers, in particular, W. C. Robinson at Columbia Theological Seminary, E. T. Ramsdell and Roy Battenhouse at Vanderbilt University School of Religion, and Albert Outler, Roland Bainton, and Robert L. Calhoun at Yale University Divinity School. I owe a debt to fellow ministers and to a host of students, too large a group to mention but crucially important to me both personally and in my understanding of the work of the ministry. They know who they are. I need not mention them here. I am grateful, above all, to them.

I owe much to the institutions in which I have taught and to my colleagues. I have always been close to an excellent library. Much of my work has been made possible by the Union Theological Seminary Library and the assistance I received from Martha Aycock Suggs, who was Research Librarian and Assistant Librarian, and from William Harris and his assistants, especially Raymond Cannata, of the Princeton Theological Seminary Library.

A considerable part of the work on this book was done while I was at White Memorial Presbyterian Church in Raleigh, North Carolina, which provided me an office and also the secretarial support of Rebecca Turner. Betty Gilbert provided secretarial help while I was on the staff of Peachtree Presbyterian Church. Angela Basmajian in Richmond, Virginia, typed portions of the manuscript and prepared it for the publisher. I am indebted to Peachtree Presbyterian Church in Atlanta for financing secretarial assistance for me since my retirement at Union Theological Seminary. Norma Kuhn, who did secretarial work for me when I was a professor at Union Theological Seminary, has continued to help me in many ways in my retirement. Roger Nicholson has been very helpful to me in the light of his experience in recruiting and his studies of theological education. Joe Small of the General Assembly staff was gracious in responding to my inquiries. Robert Johnson, a graduate student at Union Theological Seminary, and Greg Cruice at Columbia Theological Seminary gave support, looking up data and finding references for this volume.

I am indebted to many who talked with me about the issues discussed here and who read all or portions of the manuscript. They include W. Frank Harrington, William P. Wood, Charles Raynal, W. T. Stuart, Samuel Moffett, George Stroup, and Ann W. Leith.

I am grateful for the help I have received from Davis Perkins and Stephanie Egnotovich of Westminster John Knox Press in the editing and production of this book, and for the excellent work of Myra Alexander, copyeditor, and Carl Helmich, production editor.

I am grateful above all to the countless persons along the way of life who have contributed more to me and meant more to me than they know. They are too many to list, and furthermore many of life's most significant experiences are private. In conclusion let me say clearly that I am responsible for the judgments and the critique of church and seminary life printed in this book.

J.H.L.

Introduction

In 1933 Alfred North Whitehead wrote that until then it had been assumed that "each generation will substantially live amid conditions governing the lives of its father and that the traditions of the father would be passed on." "We are living," he concluded, "in the first period of human history for which the assumption is false."[1] This judgment has been substantiated in our society, and it is now being substantiated in our church.

The Presbyterian Church from its earliest theological origins in the Reformation in Zurich in 1519 until World War II lived according to its traditions, but after World War II radical changes began. Ministers increasingly began to wear robes. The lectionary returned. The Christian calendar, the observance of Lent and Holy Week, became part of the life of the church. The tradition of studied prayer gave way to the tradition of the read prayer. These changes, however, were not nearly as serious as the penetration of the church by the assumptions of a secular culture. Whitehead's observation can be applied to many old-line or established churches in the Western world. It is particularly true of the Presbyterian Church (U.S.A.) and its seminaries.

The quantifiable data concerning the Presbyterian Church are very depressing. In 1966 the United Presbyterian Church U.S.A. and the Presbyterian Church (U.S.) together had 4,250,000 members. In 1996 the reunited church membership had dropped to 2,665,276. In those same years the population of the United States had increased from 196,560,000 to 248,709,873 in 1990.

Other data for the same period (1966–1996) confirm the decline. Adult baptisms have declined from 29,002 to 12,979. Infant baptisms fell from 75,476 to 40,375. Church school membership likewise dropped from 2,324,507 to 1,082,591.

The number of local congregations has likewise decreased from 13,004 to 11,361. Yet the number of ministers increased from 17,094 to 20,640. The increase in ministers is the only major category that has shown an increase in the Presbyterian Church (U.S.A.). This increase combined with the decrease in the number of churches has many serious consequences, particularly in efforts to maintain unemployed or underemployed ministers in programs that are disastrous for local congregations, such as insistence on long vacancies with interim pastors.

Figure 1, an analysis of congregations and membership from 1988 to 1993, a period when the leadership of the General Assembly Council and the seminaries was unchallenged, indicates the pervasiveness of the decline.

This analysis also indicates the importance of small churches for the denomination. Seminaries, as well as church leadership, must find a way to provide the highest quality ministerial leadership for these congregations if the denomination is to recover its vitality.

The growth of the Presbyterian Church U.S. (Southern) in the first half of the twentieth century stands in sharp contrast to the recent indices of decline. The Presbyterian Church U.S. doubled in membership in the first quarter of the century and increased by 50 percent from 1925 to 1950. This increase took place during a period of two world wars and the devastating economic turbulence from 1920 to 1940.[2]

The decline in career missionaries is the most serious indicator of the crisis in the church. In 1927 the Presbyterian Church U.S.A. (Northern) had 1,606 long-term missionaries. After uniting with the United Presbyterian Church of North America, a great missionary church, the new United Presbyterian Church missionaries had declined to 1,261 in 1960 for a loss of 345. In that year the Presbyterian Church U.S. reported 477 long-term missionaries making a total of 1,738 long-term missionaries in 1960. In 1988 the combined churches had fewer than 400 missionaries including some short-term appointments for a loss of 1,338. The theological significance of this decline in missionaries is critical and devastating.

The decline in missionaries from 1,738 career missionaries in 1960 to around 400 (long-term, compensated personnel) in 1996 is a crucial

Church Size	1988 Number of Congregations	Membership	1993 Number of Congregations	Membership
(1) 2,000+	73	212,807	68	205,158
(2) 1,001–2,000	354	471,705	317	419,105
(3) 501–1,000	1,035	699,976	918	618,407
(4) 201–500	2,879	909,718	2,751	862,006
(5) 151–200	1,175	205,320	1,107	192,454
(6) 1–150	6,037	439,304	6,231	445,062
Total	11,553	2,938,830	11,392	2,742,192

FIGURE 1

Information provided by staff of General Assembly Council.

indication of the church's problem.[3] Whenever the leadership of the church and seminaries passionately believe that Jesus Christ is the word made flesh, that in Jesus Christ God has wrought the salvation of all people, that God raised Jesus from the dead, then the sending of evangelistic missionaries to proclaim the gospel and build churches becomes a high priority. Educational missions, medical missions, economic assistance all live and survive on the theological commitment.

David Barrett, in his annual statistical analysis of Christian missions in the *International Bulletin of Missionary Research* (January 1997), emphasizes the decline in mission activity among non-Christians. The failure of older foreign mission boards to place missionaries among the unevangelized can only reflect a radical change in theology, especially the understanding of what God did in Jesus Christ.

The radical decline in men for the ministry is a fact that must also be noted. In 1995–96 Presbyterian Church (U.S.A.) theological schools enrolled in their M.Div. programs 1,668 students of whom 753 were female and 915 were male. The total figure, enhanced by a great increase in female students, obscures the decline in male students, especially young white male students. The figures become alarming when the enrollment of particular institutions is analyzed. In 1960 Union Theological Seminary in Virginia had 231 Bachelor of Divinity students of whom 3 were female. In 1996 Union had 99 Master of Divinity students of whom 43 were women. Male students declined from 238 in 1960 to 56 in 1996. In 1960 Columbia Seminary had 172 male students in the Bachelor of Divinity program. In 1996 Columbia Seminary had 149 Master of Divinity students of whom 64 were women. Male students declined from 172 to 85. Princeton Theological Seminary in 1960–61 had 319 Bachelor of Divinity students of whom at least 5 were women. In 1996 Princeton Seminary had 403 Master of Divinity students of whom 145 were women. The number of male students had decreased from 314 to 258. When the ethnic ratios are factored in, it is likely that the decline in young white male students will be revealed to be even more serious.[4]

The refusal of the church generally to take these indications of decline seriously is more significant than the decline itself. There has been no evident concern on the part of the bureaucratic and political leaders of the church over the past thirty years about the indices of decline. The declining figures have been observed in passing, but they have not led to any specific and major action to remedy them.

There is no embarrassment over failed policies, decisions, and programs by the persons who have been responsible for them. In fact the response of the leadership of the church, as in the Minneapolis Re-imagining Conference crisis, has been full speed ahead with the policies that have led to this crisis.

It is important to note that the church as well as the American Association of Theological Schools has a great proclivity to seek university-based persons to advise on theological crises and problems over against persons more oriented to the pastorate or those who combine scholarship and the pastorate. The consequence is that the crisis has not been honestly faced in church or seminary.

The seminaries are deeply involved in the crisis of the church. The crisis itself is sufficient indication that the seminaries are not graduating ministers who are effective leaders in the life of the church. Why should it be otherwise, when seminary faculties no longer include persons who have been effective pastors themselves? The dossiers of seminary faculty members will in many instances indicate pastoral experience. Yet when the fine print is read, this is usually for a brief time, or supply work, or as associate pastors. There are virtually no faculty who have given leadership in the building of churches. Every faculty should include a few professors who through their own efforts have brought into the life of the church a sufficient *net* number of persons whose contributions would pay their salary and expense accounts.

The understanding of the church and the ministry has likewise changed on seminary campuses and among Presbyterians generally. Many seminary students seem to think of the church as an institution like General Motors that has so many jobs to which they are entitled. The old image of fifty years ago was that the church provided young ministers an opportunity to create their own "jobs" by gathering congregations and building them up.

The ethos of a Baptist seminary, as I have experienced it recently, is very different. Baptist students know that if they can go out and give leadership in bringing people into the membership of the church, in persuading people to worship God, and in raising a budget, they have a work to do as a pastor. If they cannot give this leadership, they do not expect the church to take care of them.

The most serious focus of the crisis in the church may well be a generation of Presbyterian ministers taught by seminary faculties lacking the experience of being effective pastors and under curriculum and educational policies that did not force them to master the biblical and theological competencies that enable them to do serious theological reflection on the issues before the church. This failure in education when combined with the pressures of political correctness and social orthodoxies undermines the capacity of ministers to think for themselves and to take public stands on issues before the church. The consequence is that too many church leaders and ministers are subject to being blown about by every wind of doctrine and every fad, lacking a clear identity and the power of self-determination.

The crisis in the church and the crisis in the seminary are closely related. Each has been distracted from its primary task in mission by the enticements of a secular and cause-oriented society. The church has too frequently forgotten that it lives by the gospel of what God has done for our salvation, not by what human beings have achieved. It has been bewitched by the optimism of an Enlightenment society and by inordinate confidence in what it can do for its own salvation and for the world. It has been enticed by causes, causes good in themselves, but when they become inordinate are self-destructive. No one can doubt the importance of the causes of peace, of justice, of the dignity and rightful opportunities for women, of the environment, of good race relations. Yet human achievements are always broken and fragmentary. We cannot save ourselves by what we ourselves can do. History cannot complete itself. Our causes for which we live, as H. Richard Niebuhr knew, all die.[5] Augustine learned this long ago. Having been bewitched in his early years by the achievements of Rome, he came in his final days to understand that Rome too would vanish. Our only security is in God.

The seminary, like the church, has been bewitched by causes ranging from the feminist movement to the environment. It has been enticed by the possibilities of therapy and social engineering. It has too frequently forgotten that the church lives by what God does, not by what human beings do. The church is not the Redeemer, God is the Redeemer.

The legacies of Deism, of the Enlightenment, and of Troeltschian historicism in seminary communities have undercut the conviction that God is personal and that God works personally in the created orders of history. Yet the church lives by what the personal God has done for us and for our salvation, by the conviction that God has acted for us in Jesus Christ, who is the truth and the action of God.

In the traditional Presbyterian seminary, the Bible was never simply a piece of Near Eastern literature, but the inspired word of God. The heart of the gospel has never been what human beings can do, but what God has done and is doing for our salvation.

The action of the 1996 General Assembly of the Presbyterian Church (U.S.A.), giving Commissioned Lay Pastors the right to administer the sacraments, to moderate session meetings, and to vote in presbytery, if approved by the presbyteries, reverses a consistent Presbyterian emphasis for almost three centuries in this country on an educated ministry. This action is rooted partially in the seminary's lost contact with congregational life, especially in the decline in the traditional fieldwork programs in which seminary students did what lay pastors now do. If this proposal is adopted, it will have significant consequences not only for the life of the Presbyterian Church and for Presbyterian polity, but also for the seminaries, whose role will be changed or diminished. The action concerning Commissioned Lay Pastors may not resolve the problems the Presbyterian Church is facing today. The test will finally be the same for lay pastors as it is for seminary graduates, namely, whether lay pastors can give leadership in increasing church membership, participation in worship and stewardship.

The way out of the crisis, either in the church or in theological seminaries, is difficult to outline. In institutional life as well as in communal life, it is always easier to get into a problem than it is to get out. Bureaucratic structures are hard to change. In the short run, bureaucratic structures have even more power than money has. They do not have to answer to anyone, especially when they live on endowments. In theological seminaries there is now the added problem of tenure, defined according to secular standards. In my own experience I have learned there are no unimportant appointments. Every appointment to a tenured position has long-range consequences, some unintended.

The solution to the crisis will not come from committee meetings, faculty retreats, or public relations pronouncements of what are now called offices of institutional advancement. Concerning this we can be certain. Committee meetings and retreats are frequently ways of escaping the problem, not ordinarily a way of solving the problem. Committees relieve individuals of the responsibility of making decisions and of being accountable.

Professor Albert Outler, who taught in three universities, once said that on the basis of his experience, the only effective pressure on faculties is peer pressure. Faculties, for example, keep regular office hours or participate in worship where there is peer pressure to do so, not by virtue of a rule or regulation. This is all the more true in the more important matters of theological and church commitment.

Changes will occur in our theological seminaries only when the hearts and minds of faculty are changed and when the personal commitments of newly appointed faculty are important considerations in the appointments. Some directions for the seminaries are clear. More faculty must be appointed out of the constituency which the seminary serves, whose identity is compatible with the identity of that constituency. More faculty members are needed whose primary identity is that of a Presbyterian minister or for whom this identity is far more important than academic identity. Some on every faculty should have demonstrated real effectiveness as pastors. In fact, every faculty ought to have at least one person who has brought into the membership of the church a *net* number of people whose contributions would pay the salary and expense account of the faculty member. Until a minister or a faculty member has been effectively involved in such an increase in church membership and therefore in giving, that person is living on the labors of those who have gone before.

The most important question is theological. It is the question of the Gospels (Luke 9:20), what do you think of Jesus Christ? All people must pray, "Lord, I believe; help thou mine unbelief" (Mark 9:24). Yet seminaries ought to be communities, not of people struggling to find faith, or in therapy, but communities in which faculty have committed themselves to faith in Jesus Christ as God Incarnate, the Word made flesh (John 1:14). This must be the intention and, at least in a broken and fragmentary way, the passionate commitment of every faculty member. Changes will occur in theological seminaries only when faculties passionately believe that Jesus Christ is the Word made flesh (John 1:14), that Jesus Christ is the wisdom and the power of God (1 Corinthians 1:24), that God raised Jesus from the dead who then confronted his disciples, speaking to them and commissioning them to go into all the world to teach and preach, making disciples of all people (Act 3:15; Matthew 28:19–20). This passionate faith must be more evident on seminary faculties than passion about the issues of political correctness or the issues of a secular society. The crisis in the seminary faculty, as in the church's ministry in general, is finally personal and theological.

1

The Crisis

The crisis in the life of the church and in the seminaries has been long in the making, at least for the last three decades. It is also coextensive with the entire life of the organized church. Hence, no neat, simple outline of the crisis is possible. It is complex and deeply rooted.

Three dimensions of the crisis were clearly outlined in Jeffrey Hadden's *The Gathering Storm in the Churches,* published in 1969. The crisis involved belief, purpose, and orientation of persons in the organizational leadership of the church. Another dimension of the crisis can be documented in the rise and collapse of evangelical liberalism as an effective theological movement in the life of the church. These two dimensions of the crisis are not an exhaustive list, but they do indicate some of the basic problems that arise today in the life of the church and in the seminaries.

An Analysis

In 1969 Jeffrey Hadden declared that the churches faced a crisis rooted in three causes: (1) a crisis of belief, (2) confusion as to the mission of the church, (3) a new professional class of church bureaucrats who were not closely related to the church on the congregational level.[1] This analysis has proved to be clinically exact for mainline churches. It is also a reasonably good description of what has happened to the church's seminaries.

The seminaries do face a crisis of belief. Many basic Christian doctrines are at risk on seminary campuses today. Furthermore, there is little evidence of any passionate proclamation of the foundational convictions of Christian faith or of the Christian gospel of what God has done for the salvation of human beings. Passionate convictions do exist on seminary campuses, but they frequently find their most vigorous expression in the advocacy of causes such as the agenda of the feminist movement, or the black caucus, or left-wing political organizations. There is little evidence that seminary faculties have a similar passion for proclaiming the foundational doctrines of Christian faith in a secular age. They censor chapel speakers as to the political correctness of their language but not as to the orthodoxy or integrity of their theology.

Seminary professors and seminary communities do render their testimonies today, but their testimonies have to do more with their political convictions than they do with the actions of God for our salvation. There is little evidence of a similar passion for "saving souls," for organizing or nurturing churches, for worldwide missions proclaiming Jesus Christ in order to bring persons to confess him as Lord and Savior and to build congregations.

Faculties today differ radically from the faculties of forty to fifty years ago. In 1960 there were seventeen members of the faculty at Union Theological Seminary in Virginia, and of these all except two were graduates of Union Seminary. In September 1996, of the nineteen full-time tenurable faculty only three were Union Theological Seminary graduates, including the librarian and the president. What has happened at Union Theological Seminary has happened at many other institutions. Increasingly faculties are chosen from Ph.D applicants who have been educated in secular universities. Seminary faculties are now strongly identified with professional organizations. They no longer come to the extent they once did out of the organized life of the church, and virtually none of the contemporary seminary faculties has a record of distinguished achievement as a pastor.

The consequence is that theological seminaries are no longer seen as primarily institutions for the training of pastors, but as institutes for the discussion and study of religion. A new type of professor inevitably moves the seminary in a new direction away from the task of educating people to establish congregations. In view of the fact that most faculty members themselves have never built churches, this development is all the more understandable.

The seminaries as well as denominational leadership easily forget that the primary form of the church is the congregation that gathers to hear the Word of God and to praise God and that lives in fellowship.

The three changes that Hadden finds as the cause of the malaise of the churches are also the cause of the malaise of the seminaries and of the inability of seminaries to educate effective pastors. The problem of the seminary is (1) a crisis of belief, (2) confusion as to mission, and (3) a new type of professor chosen outside the seminary constituency.

The Rise and Collapse
of Evangelical Liberalism

The crisis in the Presbyterian Church (U.S.A.) can also be described in terms of the collapse of liberalism as a productive theological and ecclesiastical commitment. Evangelical liberalism came as a liberating spirit into the Presbyterian churches of the 1930s and 1940s. As a student in high school, and later as a college student, I listened with enthusiasm each Sunday afternoon to Harry Emerson Fosdick's radio sermons and frequently ordered copies of them with a penny postcard. Later my own theological development was enhanced by Professor Robert Calhoun's articulation of the Christian faith on this side of the Enlightenment and in an idiom understandable to modern people. Professor Calhoun was a decisive theological influence in two of the finest theological statements to come out of the ecumenical movement: "The Relation of the Church to the War in the Light of the Christian Faith," produced by a committee of the Federal Council of Churches, and the theological statement on hope that was prepared for the Evanston meeting of the World Council of Churches. Francis Pickens Miller, a former executive of the World's Student Christian Federation and a member of the committee to prepare the statement on hope, once commented to me that Robert Calhoun was the only person to whose theological judgment he had ever seen Karl Barth defer. The evangelical liberals maintained their life theologically alongside the new Reformation theology and the biblical theology movement.

Liberalism gained dominance in the ecclesiastical structure of the church in the 1960s controlling all the bureaucratic machinery of the church. Liberals had also gained control in many colleges and were increasing their influence in theological seminaries. After the mid-sixties, the old brand of right-wing theology did not dominate any of the organizational structures or the institutions of the church.

Theological liberalism at the moment of its ascendancy began to lose its critical capacity. It was no longer primarily a spirit and a method. It had become a doctrinaire position and a means of self-identification. Reinhold Niebuhr once commented that sin for a liberal was to be outflanked on the left. I remember talking to ministers in the 1960s who were somehow worried that they had not moved far enough to the left. In doing so, liberalism significantly changed.

Theological liberalism, having survived the new Reformation theology and the biblical theology movement, was unable to deal with the radical left. Having lost its capacity for critical judgment, it followed the radical left not only in theological matters but also in support of policies and procedures in the church, though these were obviously not productive of church growth and strength.

It is significant to note that while Harry Emerson Fosdick and Robert Calhoun were known as the great evangelical liberals of the 1930s and 1940s they would today in any theological seminary with which I am familiar be regarded as conservative. In the 1930s and 1940s a person on the right wing of the theological spectrum affirmed biblical inerrancy and insisted, for example, on the importance of the virgin birth as a historical fact for the integrity of Christian faith. Today a conservative in a contemporary theological environment is a person who believes in a personal God, working personally in the created orders of history and nature, who believes that Jesus Christ is the embodiment of the wisdom and the power of God, who believes that God really raised Jesus Christ from the dead, and who still affirms eternal life.

Theological liberalism in the practical life of the church lost its capacity to evaluate policies and began to affirm uncritically the ideological programs of self-styled liberal groups. Liberals approved too easily any program claiming to be on behalf of the oppressed, or for social justice, or for the rights of minorities, ethnic groups, or women. Liberalism also lost its capacity to bring any critical judgment out of the classical Christian tradition to bear on the most extreme denials of classical Christian faith as, for example, at the Minneapolis Re-imagining Conference (1993).

Liberalism, which began as a theological spirit and method and which brought freedom to the theology of the church, now lost its capacity for critical theological judgments and wisdom in guiding the church. Theological liberalism was done in, not by the conservatives, not even by new Reformation theology or biblical theology, but by its inability to respond critically to the demands of the radical left.

Consequences of the Crisis

The consequences of these developments can be enumerated with some clarity.

Loss of Tradition

Church seminaries were established in the first half of the nineteenth century by particular church communities, by presbyteries and synods, for the specific purpose of educating pastors. The seminaries grew out of the life of the church for the service of the church.

The seminaries originally incorporated the theology of the church into their own theology and practice. They taught the theology that had nurtured the churches, and the theology that the seminaries taught was demonstrably able to organize, nurture, and gather churches.

The seminaries understood they belonged to a clearly defined tradition beginning with Huldrych Zwingli and John Calvin and developing through the scholastic theologians, the Puritan revolution and the Westminster Assembly, Heinrich Heppe and Charles Hodge, and more recently Emil Brunner and Karl Barth. The basic theological texts used in the seminaries were those that had received the *approbation* of the people of God in the Presbyterian Church, namely, the theologies of Francis Turretin, Charles Hodge, and others.

Tradition is more than theology. It is also ethos, practice, and life. The seminary faculties were drawn out of the life of the church; that is, out of the constituency of the seminary for which it was educating pastors. They brought with them to the campus the life, the practices, and the ethos of the church's life. The seminary then was determined by the church.

Today seminaries are shaped more by graduate schools that are frequently parts of secular universities. Faculties are increasingly concerned about membership in the numerous professional organizations that exist today. They do not bring to their teaching a similar sense of accountability to the church or even the same sense of being as at home in the church as in the professional organization.

The seminaries have lost their depth in time and history. Seminaries that had very distinguished faculties in the nineteenth century have today forgotten those faculties. In 1860 Columbia Theological Seminary had on its faculty and in its surrounding community as able a group of ministers and teachers as had ever been assembled in American Presbyterianism except around Princeton. In the nineteenth century Princeton Theological Seminary shaped American church life as did no other seminary. No nineteenth-century American theologian was as influential in the life of Christian communities as was Charles Hodge.

The three seminaries I know best, Columbia, Union Theological Seminary in Virginia, and Princeton demonstrate little pride in or memory of their past. They seem to prefer to operate in the present without tradition. Mark Noll has written more extensively and appreciatively of Princeton theology than any member of the current Princeton faculty.[2] No faculty member at Columbia Theological Seminary since W. C. Robinson (Columbia Seminary professor, 1926–1967) has written as appreciatively of the Columbia theological heritage as has Eugene Genovese in *The Southern Front* and other writings.[3]

In *Reformed Theology in America: A History of Its Modern Developments,* edited by David S. Wells (1986), George Marsden, W. Andrew Hoffecker, and others have claimed Princeton theology for Reformed communities not only outside the orbit of Princeton Theological Seminary but also outside the Presbyterian Church (U.S.A.). Other writers in this volume made the same claim for the theological traditions at Union Theological Seminary and at Columbia Theological Seminary.[4]

It is significant that the writings of nineteenth-century Presbyterian theologians are continually being reprinted, though they are seldom to be found on mainline seminary bibliographies or in Presbyterian seminary bookstores. Nine of Charles Hodge's ten books are currently in print, sometimes from several different publishers, 118 years after his death. Four books by A. A. Hodge (1879–1886) are available and at least four volumes of Archibald Alexander, the first professor at Princeton, are also available along with five volumes from Joseph Alexander, who taught at Princeton from 1833 to 1860. Thirteen volumes of Benjamin B. Warfield's (1887–1920) works are currently available as well as the ten-volume set of his collected works that is kept in print by

Baker Book House. Five books of Robert L. Dabney (1820–1888) are in print as well as James Henley Thornwell's (1812–1862) four-volume collected work and smaller individual publications. Sprinkle Printing Company of Harrisonburg, Virginia, has recently published three volumes from John L. Girardeau (Columbia Theological Seminary professor, 1876–1895). This list of Presbyterian publications from the faculties of Columbia, Princeton, and Union in the nineteenth century is not complete, but it is sufficient to indicate that the theological heritage of these three institutions is very much alive today, but not on those campuses. This listing also points to a widespread Reformed community in America that is not noticed by mainline Presbyterian seminaries. Yet it was the theology that was contained in these volumes that built Princeton, Union, and Columbia seminaries as well as the church community of which they are a part.[5]

The loss of tradition in the seminaries contributes to the loss of tradition in local congregations. A recent study by Phillip Hammond concludes that "church" no longer means what it did a few decades ago. People go to church less out of habit and less out of participation in the collective way of life of a people or tradition. They go to church to carry out their own purposes and to assert their personally constructed religious views. They expect the church to meet their needs, as they have defined them.[6]

Loss of Gratitude

Loss of tradition leads to loss of gratitude. Those who do not remember cannot be thankful for all that is bequeathed to them.

Every church building stands because of the labors of ministers and church members, sometimes at great sacrifice, sometimes at great risk, demanding courage, and sometimes with great vision among people with little vision. Congregations do not just happen. Someone not only preached but went out into the byways and hedges and brought people into the church. The cannibalization of congregations by people, including ministers who did not build them, is a serious problem in contemporary church life. Church leadership, unfortunately, can live parasitically for a number of years on churches and institutions they did not build.

Institutions, including seminaries, are not immune from the exploitation of the resources that have been bequeathed from the past.

The problem is not simply living off resources that one did not earn, but using those resources for purposes that contradict the purposes of those who built the institutions and endowed them.

The absence of memory on the part of contemporary faculties of those whose work made possible the institutions in which they now teach is a problem not only of policy but also of morality. What moral right does a faculty have to use resources that they did not provide, for purposes that contradict the purposes of those who built the institution? The prophetic ministry on seminary campuses begins with the responsible use of what has been bequeathed from the past.

Every minister accepting a call to a congregation, every professor accepting a call to a seminary, every seminary administrator, and every trustee of a seminary ought to apply to his or her work the words of Deuteronomy 6:10–12:

> When the Lord your God has brought you into the land that he swore to your ancestors, to Abraham, to Isaac, and to Jacob, to give you—a land with fine, large cities that you did not build, houses filled with all sorts of goods that you did not fill, hewn cisterns that you did not hew, vineyards and olive groves that you did not plant—and when you have eaten your fill, take care that you do not forget the Lord, who brought you out of the land of Egypt, out of the house of slavery.

George Buttrick, a great minister of a previous generation, in a chapel address at Union Theological Seminary advised seminarians on going to a congregation to ponder these words of Deuteronomy and to be grateful for the labors of those who had given so much to them. He also advised, in words now strange in the contemporary "call" system, not to attempt to take over the work of God in seeking calls.[7]

Loss of Church Orientation—Secularization

The loss of tradition and the loss of an intimate connection with the organized life of the church have led to secularization. Secularization of the seminary campus appears in many ways. First of all, it is found in the administrative structures of the seminaries, which now do not differ in any significant way from those of secular institutions. The tremendous increase in seminary administration has been one of the characteristic changes in seminary life in recent years. Secularization is also reflected in pay schedules that reward administrators more than professors. In the 1950s Benjamin R. Lacy, president of Union Theological Seminary in Virginia, received the same salary as senior faculty. James A. Jones who followed President Lacy received only a slightly higher salary. Benjamin Lacy and James Jones were as effective seminary presidents as any institution ever had. The significant increase in executive salaries has not increased the effectiveness of the office. Furthermore, no *theological* reason has been found to justify higher salaries for administrators of modest achievements than, for example, for a New Testament professor with an international reputation.

Secularization penetrates not only administration but also campus life generally. Unless present trends are reversed it is likely that campus life on a seminary campus will be less and less distinguishable from campus life on any secular educational campus.

The secularization of the seminaries is also to be found in their dependence on secular accrediting agencies that may impose policies and procedures that undermine the seminary's purpose, for example, a secular tenure policy that requires a seminary to continue a professor whose teaching undermines the life of the church. The review that determines whether or not a seminary is approved is done not by the church but by secular organizations.

Loss of Sense of Mission and Direction

Seminaries, as has been stated, were established by the church to prepare pastors for the church. Contemporary faculties coming out of graduate schools tend to pressure the seminaries in another direction; namely, that of the academic institution. Seminary faculties increasingly like to think of themselves as centers for thought, for research, for the writing of articles and books and creative theological enterprises.

This development in theological seminaries has been accelerated by the inflation of Ph.D.'s. Graduate schools granting Ph.D.'s in religion have greatly increased in number. Moreover, the publication of books and articles has become increasingly easy in that funds are made available to subsidize the cost. While there is undoubtedly justification for the subsidization of the publishing of certain books that will not have much sale but are critically important for the life and work of the church, the practice of publishing books that have no reason to sell has serious consequences. There is little value in publishing books or articles unless they advance knowledge or enhance the life of the church.

The emphasis on publishing, on going to professional meetings, and on teaching graduate students has diverted the attention of seminary faculties from their primary task which is preparing persons to be effective pastors of local congregations.

Loss of Curriculum Focus on the Congregation

Curriculum revision has been endemic in theological education since World War II. Fifty years ago curricula were very simple: Bible, history, theology including ethics, and pastoral theology. With greatly enlarged faculties has come a necessity for an increased number of courses to accommodate the special interests of faculty.

The great proliferation of courses, particularly in the pastoral field, in areas dictated by the political and social agendas of secular society and in narrow fields of scholarship has detracted from competence in the basic fields of theological learning. Less time is available in the curriculum for basic theological education in Bible and the church's theology. The globalization of theological study may be in itself a good emphasis, but it can also shift the focus of theological education from the preparation of pastors for the calls that are likely to come to them.

Moreover, theology and biblical studies as well as history are becoming increasingly professional and technical. When professional and technical scholarship is added to the decline in hours available for basic training in theology, Bible, and history, it is very difficult for students to leave the seminaries today with as great a knowledge of the biblical texts or the history of the church or the theology of the church as they did in former years.

The task of the seminary is not to produce church historians, professional theologians, or technical biblical scholars. The first task is to prepare preachers who use theological and biblical knowledge to proclaim the gospel and to nurture congregations.

Theological students today no doubt graduate from seminaries with a greater knowledge in highly specialized fields of study, but it is safe to say that many graduate without having read the Bible through from Genesis to Revelation and without knowing, in a systematic way, the theology of the confessions and the church. Many students graduate having read a few pages of many theologians, but without having mastered any comprehensive theological text that played a decisive role in the growth and development of American Presbyterianism.

Loss of
Ecclesiastical Commitment

The religious studies enterprises have increasingly made use of the churches for their own good. This is especially true of departments of religion in colleges and universities. It is not likely that departments of religion would have many students apart from the interest created by the life of the church. The vitality of the work of historical critics, as well as the attention the Jesus Seminar receives in newspapers, depends on the vitality of religious communities, who believe that the Bible is more than a piece of Near Eastern literature.[8]

Many believed in the late 1940s and early 1950s that with the development of religion departments, especially in state universities, the life of the church would be greatly enriched. There is little evidence to justify that today.

Fifty years ago departments of Bible in church colleges taught courses not simply to instruct or to encourage discussion but to enhance Christian life in the church. Today the situation is different. College courses in religion taught in a value neutral context with no "privileged" text or religion undermine the life of the church more than they build it up. In fact the university context is seldom neutral. It may actually be anti-Christian, and Christian texts may be interpreted by a "hermeneutics" of suspicion.

The seminaries have not been immune from the academic exploitation of the church. Seminaries would not exist apart from the support of the churches that founded them and have sustained them. Whenever faculties use their position in theological seminaries primarily for academic purposes and for purposes that do not enrich the life of the church, they become exploiters of the church.

Loss of Accountability

The loss of accountability has two roots: (1) Some Presbyterian seminaries have severed all ties with church governing bodies and are freestanding institutions with self-perpetuating boards. Most Presbyterians are unaware of the change to self-perpetuating boards and no one talks about the consequences of these changes ten to twenty years in the future. (2) Seminaries are not scrutinized by an independent press as secular universities are.

Presbyterians know more about their state universities than they do about their seminaries. Knowledge of the seminaries and of what goes on in seminary board meetings and on the campuses of seminaries is largely limited to public relations releases. Most seminaries today publish expensive promotional literature, but this is designed to win friends and influence people, not to subject the seminary to serious reporting.

It is much easier to learn the salaries of administrators and faculties of state universities than to know the salaries of seminary administrators and faculties. The newspapers cover the actual debates in board meetings and controversies on the campus of state universities. No similar scrutiny is available for the church. Hence, seminaries have lost a sense of accountability both to church courts and to the judgment of church members.

Loss of Academic Freedom

The role of academic freedom in a church seminary is difficult to define. The experiences of the fundamentalist controversies left an indelible impression on the life of the church and the determination to provide on seminary campuses the freedom to exercise responsible judgment within the parameters of the seminary's commitments. Fifty years ago it was necessary to gain freedom for the study of the faith. The tragedy is that freedom *for* the faith became freedom *from* the faith.

Yet academic freedom in a seminary is difficult to define. The seminary must provide freedom to study critically the faith; yet it must do so within the boundaries of the faith. "No community," writes Jon Levenson, "can be equally open to all ideas, and the academic equivalent of the First Amendment absolutism . . . is neither possible nor desirable."[9] "An absolutist version of 'academic freedom,' " writes Geoffrey Wainwright of Duke University, "imported from the secular world that is otherwise committed only to relativism, is quite misplaced in an ecclesial institution."[10]

The irony of Presbyterian seminaries is that academic freedom permits professors to call in question basic Christian doctrines such as a

personal God or the resurrection of Jesus Christ or eternal life, but at
the same time allows no freedom to challenge the dogmas of feminist
theology. No fundamentalist group in the South was ever as relent-
less in denying freedom for theology and ministry as the left wing of
the Presbyterian Church (U.S.A.) has been in denying freedom to
those who challenge their special dogmas, not only in the seminary
but in the church. The left-wing censors leave few openings for freedom. They demand that new appointments to faculties respect their
dogmas, and they even attempt to censor the language of chapel
speakers. Princeton, Union in Virginia, and Columbia all have statements in their handbooks specifying the "inclusive" language they
expect of chapel speakers. Yet the same left wing supported the use
of crude and vulgar language at the Minneapolis Re-imagining Conference, such as specific sexual references not usually heard in church
gatherings as well as crude caricatures of traditional Christian doctrines such as the atonement.

Seminaries provide freedom for the radical criticism of Christian
doctrine. Yet there is no freedom to criticize the new dogmas of political correctness that have *not* received the approbation of Christian
people on the congregational level. This is the tragedy of seminary
life today.

The pressure from the orthodoxies of political correctness and social agendas endangers the integrity of theological scholarship. Theological work is now done with the author greatly concerned with the
censors. Hence serious theological work may become at least in part
a political tract giving the social location of the author by the use of
code words and clichés as well as deliberate theological judgments
that will satisfy the demands of social, fad, and politically correct orthodoxies.[11] Furthermore, many writers so load their theological
work with the chaff of the study and answers to all available positions
that their own positive statement is obscured—in an apparent effort
to satisfy pedantic academic demands.

Loss of the Ability of Seminaries
to Educate Graduates Who Are Effective Pastors

The loss of the mainline churches in membership and the decline
of other quantifiable data indicate that something is seriously wrong.
The seminaries have to face the question of whether or not they are

educating people with the ability to go out and build churches. The obvious fact is that not many seminary graduates are doing that, even though Americans are more religious today perhaps than they have ever been in their history, and even though many local congregations are growing.

The seminaries now have faculties made up almost exclusively of persons who have no distinguished record as pastors. The question can rightly be raised whether faculties made up of persons who have never demonstrated the ability to organize, nurture, and develop a local congregation can prepare students for this important task.

The decline in the number of young men entering the seminary also poses a serious problem with grave consequences for the future. An adequate number of men as ministers is by all statistical data, I know, and in terms of church records thus far, essential for the growth of the church.

The significant increase in the number of women in the ministry is no adequate answer to the decline of men. Gender does affect the work of the minister. No ideological commitments can nullify the significance of gender differences in the work of a pastor of a church. It is as serious to ignore the significance of gender differences in the work of the ministry, as it is serious to deny the theological justification for ordaining women.

The apostle Paul declared that in Christ we are neither bond nor free, Greek nor barbarian, male nor female but one in him (Galatians 3:27–28; Colossians 3:11). The medieval church knew this when it insisted that faith creates the deepest unity or greatest division among human beings. We are one in Christ. This is the foundation. Yet human beings are still bond or free, Greek or barbarian, male and female. Unity in Christ does not erase the stubborn facts of class, of culture, of gender, and of age that is embedded in the very physical constitution of human beings.

Ordination is rightly open to people without regard to class, culture, or gender. Yet in insisting on openness to ordination the church cannot ignore the significance of class, culture, gender, and age in their impact on the work of the ministry. The church is today under ideological pressures to deny or ignore the significance for effective work in the ministry of (1) gender difference embedded in the human constitution, (2) the difference between being a mother and a father, (3) the difficulties of two-career families, and (4) the problems

posed by clergy couples. The seminaries as well as the church need to
be honest in facing these issues. Otherwise the church, meaning local congregations and the ministers themselves, will have to deal with
the problems on an ad hoc basis to the detriment of all. Mary Midgley, a British philosopher, has cogently argued that ignoring the stubborn facts of gender differences does in the end great damage to
women themselves.[12] For these reasons also mainline seminaries cannot for long ignore the decline in young white males for the ministry.

The decline of men in the ministry parallels the declining numbers
of men in church membership and the decline in the number of men
of outstanding achievement in positions of leadership in the church
on every level of governing bodies and on church boards. The basic
concern is not male or female as such. The real test is the ability to
organize churches, to bring members into the church, to raise budgets, and to give leadership in teaching and pastoral care.[13]

Church policy is too often based on what committees or persons
in leadership positions think ought to be rather than on what is. If differences of gender, race, class, culture, or age ought not to make a difference in the effectiveness of a minister in the particular situation, the
stubborn fact is that these factors always do make a difference. People
do not come to church because they ought to come, but because they
are persuaded to come. Modern people no longer fear hell, and social
pressure to come to church is weak in a secular society. Ancient people did not listen to the apostle Paul because they ought to have listened to him but because he persuaded them to listen. Some whom
Paul could not persuade Peter and Barnabas did persuade to listen.

No sermon has universal appeal except on a very basic level. Sermons that move people in one cultural or social context do not move
others in another context. Hymns that are meaningful to some mean
little to others. These differences are rooted in gender, class, culture,
race, and age. As a pastor in a college town I knew that my sermons
had no appeal for many people with no intellectual concerns and with
little concern for the impact of Christian faith on the social and political life of the community. Moreover, many people in Auburn did
not appreciate the hymns that we regularly sang in the Presbyterian
church or the music that the organist played. I was glad there were
other congregations and other preachers who could meet the needs of
persons who were equally precious in the sight of God, but who did
not like the sermons, hymns, and public witness of the Presbyterian

church in the community. Ignoring human differences is as disastrous as denying the unity in Christ, as Reinhold Niebuhr noted long ago. Culture, class, race, gender, and age all influence the work any minister is able to do in particular situations.

Seminaries no longer seriously ask, as they did in the past, if their graduates have the ability to serve as ministers. Yet ministers are not called or paid to be Christian or prophetic. This is the work of Christians as Christians. The minister is responsible for critically important functions that are essential for the growth and witness of the church. The minister must be a person who can organize and gather congregations, add members to the church, raise church budgets, and lead the church membership in the work of the church. Unless ministers can perform these functions well, the life of the congregation deteriorates.

Some may protest that this emphasis on production undercuts the witness of the minister as a preacher of the Word. This may in some cases be true. But no minister who is the beneficiary of a good salary and benefits and no presbytery that functions, as Aubrey Brown, editor of the *Presbyterian Outlook* from 1943 to 1978, has so sharply stated, as a trade union can protest an emphasis on production.[14] Seminary administrations, faculties, and church bureaucracies as well as ministers must learn that if you enjoy the fruits of production, you must produce.

2

The Boundaries
of Christian Faith

A re there any boundaries to Christian faith? This question is now critical for the church if it is to maintain its identity and integrity. For some there seem to be no boundaries. The Divine Spirit works throughout creation and history illuminating special individuals such as Jesus. The universe is somehow revelatory of its being. Persons who are moved by the Spirit can claim they are Christian even if they have no connection with the historic faith of the church.[1] Even for some in the church there is no higher authority than "feeling reality." If I feel it, experience it, it is true. This is the impact of our secular culture.

The Question of Boundaries

The question about boundaries is also answered in the negative by those who remember the unpleasantness of the fundamentalist-modernist controversies of the first half of this century. Fundamentalist has become a very pejorative word, and the implicit assumption is that it is better to have no boundaries than to attempt to set boundaries to the faith.

The problem of boundaries that is endemic in our culture comes to sharp focus in the theological seminary faculty, curriculum, and witness. Are there theological boundaries for an institution that prepares people to be ministers in Christian churches? Are there boundaries for those who seek to educate ministers for Presbyterian churches? For at least four decades Presbyterian seminaries have been reluctant to face these questions, yet these questions persist. Is there really such a thing as "the faith that was once for all entrusted to the saints" (Jude 3)?

Within the Presbyterian tradition the question has been debated from the time John Calvin forced Sebastianus Castellio to give up teaching in Geneva because of his views on the canon of scripture. For Calvin there were boundaries and the canon of scripture set one of them.[2] Within the Presbyterian tradition the controversy was most severe in the seventeenth, eighteenth, and nineteenth centuries concerning subscription. What does it mean to accept the substance of doctrine taught in the Westminster Confession of Faith? With the adoption in the Presbyterian Church (U.S.A.) of a *Book of Confessions,* the question becomes even more difficult than when the confessional commitment was limited to one creed.

The best answer that was given to the question of boundaries during the subscription controversies was that of A. A. Hodge.[3] The acceptance of the Westminster Confession, Hodge wrote, meant that one is in theology, (1) a Catholic, (2) a Protestant, (3) a Reformed theologian. This has been a very satisfactory answer, for it removes the question from the minutia of theology and centers it on the fundamental issues.

The boundary of Catholic Christianity is the Nicene Creed and the doctrine of the Trinity. The Nicene Creed and the doctrine of the Trinity were incorporated in all the major Protestant confessions. The Nicene Creed is not only the most universal of Christian creeds; it is also the most important. In answer to the question, In what sense is Jesus Christ God?, it declared that Jesus Christ is of the same substance, reality as God. When one is confronted by Jesus Christ one is confronted by God, the creator of heaven and earth, insofar as God can be embodied in and expressed through a human life. The incarnation is not a human being who is devoted to God or a human being searching for the truth or a human being who is the best and brightest of all human beings. The incarnation means that Jesus Christ is the truth (wisdom) and the action (power) of God for the salvation of all people. In many diverse ways, the writers of the New Testament attempt to say that in and through Jesus Christ God acted for our salvation and that in Jesus Christ, God himself, creator and redeemer, speaks to us.[4]

Arius in the Nicene controversy was ready to say wonderful things about Jesus, as many on the fringes of Christian faith are willing to say today. He was the best and brightest of human beings, but he was only by courtesy to be called God. The Nicene Creed summarized the faith of the church by affirming without equivocation that Jesus Christ is true God from true God, that Jesus Christ is of the same substance, essence, reality as the Father. As such the Nicene Creed is the foundational and also the universal Christian creed.

Paul Tillich has written concerning the significance of the decision of Nicaea for world history and for the history of the church: "The most serious Christian heresy was overcome. Christ is not one of many half-Gods; he is not a hero; he is God himself appearing in divine essence within an historical person. It meant a definite negation of paganism. In Arius paganism again raised its head after it had been defeated in the anti-Gnostic struggle. The victory of Arianism would have made Christianity only one of many possible religions."[5]

The Nicene theology made it imperative that the church immediately work out its doctrine of the Trinity, which was done in the East by the great Cappadocian theologians Basil the Great, Gregory of Nyssa, and Gregory of Nazianzus and in the West by the greatest of theologians Augustine. The Nicene theology also made it imperative for the church to work out the doctrine of the person of Christ, which it did at Chalcedon, setting the boundaries in which one can think about Jesus Christ. Chalcedon said that you can say what you wish about Jesus Christ, within the boundaries: (1) Jesus Christ is truly man, (2) Jesus Christ is truly God, (3) Jesus Christ is one personal subject.

The *Book of Confessions* also specifies that a Presbyterian is Protestant rather than Roman Catholic or Greek Orthodox, for example. Protestantism emphasized the doctrines of *sola scriptura, sola gratia, solus Christus*. Protestantism means the doctrines that were enunciated in Martin Luther's great writings of 1520: (1) the supreme authority of the Holy Spirit speaking through scripture in the life of the church and the world, (2) justification by grace through faith, (3) the priesthood of all believers, (4) the sanctity of the common life, (5) a clear emphasis on personal responsibility. Without faith there is no sacrament. A person does not have to be a Protestant to be a Christian, but in order to be a Presbyterian, one does have to be Protestant.

The words "Presbyterian" and "Reformed" in this context are practically interchangeable, but Presbyterian refers primarily to church polity, Reformed refers primarily to theology. A person may be Reformed theologically without being Presbyterian.

The confessions also mean that one is Reformed as well as Catholic and Protestant. Reformed theology is distinguished by its emphasis on God as action, as energy, as moral purpose, as intentionality. God is the Creator, the Lord who stretches out the heavens as a curtain, who works personally and purposefully in the created orders of nature and history. The decrees of God always played a prominent role in the theology and ethos of Reformed Christians. In contemporary language the decrees of God are the purposes of God, the divine intentionality that is the foundation of the world, of human existence and human history.

A second emphasis of Reformed theology is that the Lord God has revealed himself and that this revelation has been recorded in scripture, which is the Word of God written. The classical Reformed theologies, as well as the classical creeds, place a great emphasis on the authority of scripture, not simply on the authority of scripture for certain people in the times in which it was written, but the authority of scripture as the written Word of God for all people in all ages.

The early Reformed writings always emphasized the Lordship of God and the authority of scripture. It is difficult to see how anyone can claim to be Presbyterian and Reformed who does not on the one hand lay emphasis on the Lordship of God working personally in the created orders of history and nature and on the scriptures as the Word of God written, the final authority for life in the church.

The great question for Martin Luther was, Can God forgive sins? The question that stands behind most Reformed theology is, Has the Lord God, creator of heaven and earth, revealed himself and made himself known, and do the universe and human existence have any meaning? Reformed theology has, therefore, always been characterized by a great emphasis on the unique and decisive revelation of God in Jesus Christ and on the Bible as the Word of God written.

There are other distinctive characteristics of Reformed theology: (1) a particular way of putting together forgiveness and sanctification, (2) a distinctive way of perceiving the transcendence and immanence of God in personal terms, (3) a particular way of relating general revelation and special revelation, church and society, creation and redemption. Reformed theology has also been characterized by an emphasis on the practical rather than the theoretical, on edification rather than the vision of God. Still other characteristics of the Reformed tradition have been its emphasis on the life of the mind in the service of God and the Christian doctrine of vocation. God elects his people to be his servants *in the world*.

Many Christians share these distinctive emphases of the Reformed tradition, but taken together they represent a particular type of Christian person and community that has been historically distinguishable in Christendom.

The confessions of the Presbyterian Church set the boundaries for Presbyterians and particularly for seminary professors. Persons teaching in a seminary have traditionally been called to be authentically, genuinely, and intentionally Catholic, Protestant, and Reformed. In recent years Presbyterian seminaries have called professors from other traditions that are compatible, such as the Lutheran tradition. This has in many instances enriched theological education. Yet it must always be recognized that a Presbyterian seminary is not educating ministers in general but pastors for Presbyterian churches.

Foundational Doctrines

The church has always attempted to make a distinction between doctrines that are essential for Christian faith and ones that are not essential. While the general distinction is easy to make, its precise definition is very difficult. There is no consensus on the precise formulation of many of the doctrines that are essential to Christian faith.[6]

The fundamentalist-modernist controversies of the first half of this century fixed for the most part on many secondary doctrines. The basic doctrines were not seriously challenged. The church's existence has never been dependent on a particular doctrine of verbal inerrancy nor has it been dependent on the affirmation of the virgin birth as a historical fact. There could be a million virgin births without an incarnation. No serious person can believe Christian faith depends on an axhead floating or a talking serpent.

The doctrines that are at issue today and that are at great risk in our secular society are quite clearly not peripheral doctrines, but those that are essential for Christian faith. No Christian community has ever thrived for long without a clear affirmation of the doctrines that are precisely at risk in our society, in universities, and even in seminaries:

1. The living God who is personally and purposefully active in the created orders of history and nature
2. The revelation of God supremely in Jesus Christ and in scripture, as the Word of God written
3. The work of God for the salvation of all people in the life and death and resurrection of Jesus Christ
4. The resurrection of Jesus Christ as a reality that happened. The first disciples, using the language of ordinary experience, saw and heard the risen, crucified Jesus. They bore testimony that they were commissioned by the crucified and risen Christ to be his witness in all the world.
5. The sending of the Holy Spirit
6. The doctrine of eternal life

No Christian church in history has endured for long without the clear affirmation of these particular doctrines. All of these doctrines are clearly proclaimed in the creeds and confessions that compose the *Book of Confessions*. In the doctrinal standards of the Presbyterian Church (U.S.A.) no pluralism or diversity exists as to the faith by which the church lives and that distinguishes it from the secular culture. There is a considerable amount of evidence that the decline in mainline churches is related to the silence of mainline churches, their seminaries, and their preachers precisely on these doctrines that are at risk.[7]

The foundation of all Christian doctrines is the biblical, Catholic (Nicaea), and Protestant emphasis that God's decisive revelation has happened in history—in the call and promise to Abraham, in God's choosing a people and delivering them from Pharaoh's bondage, in the giving of the law, and above all, in the concrete historical life and death of Jesus Christ and in the witness of the disciples to his resurrection.

The emphasis on history has been increasingly replaced since Friedrich Schleiermacher by an emphasis on feeling and experience, especially in the last few decades. The revelation in history has to be modified, the new theologies of experience insist, to fit the new experiences.[8] In classical theology experience was modified and understood in the light of the revelation in history. The Holy Spirit proceeds from the Father and (through) the Son. The Holy Spirit is the Spirit of Christ.

The contemporary emphasis on experience in Presbyterian churches is a striking anomaly. Reformed Christians have always viewed expe-

rience with a critical judgment in the light of the revelation in Jesus
Christ. For this reason Reformed Christians were skeptical of the revivals, and Calvin insisted that the glory of God is more important than
the salvation of one's own soul.[9]

Contemporary theology, sometimes in the Presbyterian Church,
reverses the skepticism. Skepticism about history or the Gospel presentation of Jesus Christ has replaced skepticism about experience.
This reversal undermines classical Christianity and replaces it with a
new religion that survives only by using the old Christian words.

A second reversal is in the doctrine of God. The God in scripture
is very personal and very active in the created orders of history and
nature. In much of theology since Schleiermacher God is neither personal nor personally active in the created orders of nature and history.
Faith becomes a disposition of trust in the powers that impinge on us,
no longer trust in the Father of our Lord Jesus Christ, who is also the
Almighty Creator. The emphasis of Reformed theology on a personal, active God is reversed in modern forms of Deism or, to use the
contemporary term, panentheism.[10]

The shift in theological writings from confidence in history to confidence in experience and from a personal God to the impersonal
powers that impinge on us, but cannot be called personal, is obscured
by clever theological rhetoric so the impact is not dramatic. Yet sooner
or later the people in the pew understand, and they lose interest.

Still another shift is the modern emphasis on meaning. Calvin
never asked what the resurrection or the death of Christ meant. He
proclaimed what God had done in the death of Christ. The first question is not meaning but reality. Did it happen? When the resurrection becomes meaning, then theologians can talk about "making the
resurrection." A person of common sense with a strong perception of
reality knows a resurrection we can make is not worth bothering
about. The question is not, first, What does eternal life mean?, for example, but, "Is it a reality?"[11]

Theology, in the hands of those who no longer affirm the personal
acts of God, becomes a soporific, an aspirin tablet, to enable human
beings to endure the pain of an essentially meaningless world in
which there is no hope. Over against soporific theology, Bertrand
Russell, who no longer believed, must be admired for telling it as he
thought it was.[12]

School theology, remote from the congregation, is frequently sophisticated, clever, and pedantic. More significant, it often obscures the reality of the human situation and the concrete questions human beings ask. These questions are central to human concerns, and they are very simple but reveal a great deal about a person's theology. One such question is, Is it proper to pray for rain[13] or is it proper to pray for a cure for cancer? Another question that reveals a person's theology is, What happens that is worth talking about when a person dies? Honest answers to these questions lay bare a person's actual theological convictions. They are also the questions that people who live amid the stubborn realities of life ask. When I was a member of my presbytery's committee on examination of candidates for the ministry, I asked these questions until the word was passed that I would ask them. The questions caused consternation, though they were asked of seminary graduates.

These questions that asked if God works personally in the created orders of nature and history are crucial to the people who make up a congregation. If God is not an agent in the created order, persons who face the stubborn facts of life are not likely to think the theology or the worship informed by a minimal faith is worth either their time or their money. John Polkinghorne, a distinguished theoretical physicist, has argued that apart from a God who personally reacts to events we are without hope.[14] Theologians can work out very clever, highly imaginative theologies in their studies, but these theologies need a reality check, if a biblical check has been discarded.

Heresy

Heresy became an almost obsolete word in the life of the church in the middle decades of this century. John Macquarrie, writing in 1966, declared that "the identification and rejection of heresies were necessary and useful activities during the first five centuries in the church's experience. . . . There was always the danger of distortion or the merging of Christianity into the welter of pagan cults."[15] But the issues that justified the use of the term "heresy" were settled in the first five centuries. It is significant that at the very moment Macquarrie was making these statements, the doctrines that were beginning to be questioned in the life of the church were precisely those that the Christian community had to deal with in the first five centuries.

Heresies that the church emphatically rejected in the first five centuries now began to reappear in the writings of theologians.

Many theologians and preachers, especially in the old Presbyterian U.S. circles, grew up under the ecclesiastical oppression of radically conservative ministers and theologians and under a Victorian legalism. The supreme achievement of their lives was liberation from this "oppressive orthodoxy" and its legalism. The great tragedy is that many fail to understand that the situation has now changed. No oppressive theological orthodoxy in the life of the Presbyterian Church exists today, and neither is there any oppressive Victorian morality. Fundamentalists, as identified in the first half of the twentieth century, no longer exist in the Presbyterian Church (U.S.A.).

The actual fact is the very opposite of the older orthodoxy. No clearly defined body of beliefs inform and direct the lives of increasing numbers of young people and of middle-aged people who are now moving into the leadership of the church. No clearly outlined pattern of the Christian life dominates the life of church people and the typically Reformed practices such as the family altar and the keeping of the Lord's Day are also gone.[16] The times have changed. Yet many ministers and theologians, especially those who came to maturity in the 1950s and 1960s, speak and act as though the stabilities and commitments of church and society still provide a "safety net" as they did in the 1940s and 1950s. Hence heresy is remote from their conscious thoughts.

Jon Levenson, a Jewish scholar, in a recent article asked if there are any theological views that are regarded as heretical on liberal theological seminary campuses.[17] Professor Thomas Oden of Drew University in an article in the *Christian Century* relates heresy to the stealing of institutions. Thomas Oden's charges are easier to denounce, or rhetorically reject, as they were by a companion article in the *Christian Century,* than they are to face seriously and refute.

> An interloper who steals property must first be caught and charged. Thinly disguised atheism and neo-paganism, interlopers and "liberated" in church circles, they have engaged in the theft of church property. The stolen property must be reclaimed and the thieves brought to justice.
>
> To point this out means raising the issue of heresy. But in the "liberated" church circles of old line denominations heresy simply does not exist. After centuries of struggle against recurrent heresies,

Christians have found a quick way of overcoming heresy: they
have banished the concept altogether. With absolute relativism
holding sway, there is not only no concept of heresy, but no way
even to raise the question of where the boundaries of legitimate
Christian belief lie.

This is like trying to have a baseball game with no rules, no um-
pire, and no connection with historic baseball. . . .

By "liberated" church circles I refer to the sexual experimenters,
the compulsive planner of others' lives, canonical text disfigurers,
and ultrafeminists (as distinguished from the great company of
godly Christian women who are found at many different points
along the scale of feminist reflection). The liberated characteristi-
cally understand themselves to be free from oppressive, traditional
constraints of all sorts and shapes.[18]

Thomas Oden's charge that institutions are being stolen sounds
harsh; yet it deserves serious consideration. I first heard the word used
by Warner Hall, one of the great Presbyterian ministers of the past
generation, the pastor of Covenant Presbyterian Church in Charlotte, North Carolina, and a member of a number of boards. He
spoke out against ministers, professors, and boards that were appropriating for their own purposes institutions that they did not build.
Left-wing theological liberalism has built few, if any, great theological institutions. Left-wing theological liberalism as well as left-wing
bureaucratic leadership has maintained itself by appropriating what far
more traditional Christian believers have built and endowed. As indicated above, it is far easier to denounce what Thomas Oden has said
than to face the reality that faculties, boards, and administrative leadership as well as ministers have taken institutions that they have done
little to build and have appropriated them for their own purposes.

The claim that heretics are thieves is an ancient one. No one ever
put the case stronger than Irenaeus and especially Tertullian.

If they are heretics, they cannot be Christians, since the names
which they accept come not from Christ but from the heretics
whom they follow of their own choice. So, not being Christians,
they acquire no right to Christian literature, and we have every
right to say to them: "Who are you? When did you arrive, and
where from? You are not my people; what are you doing on my
land? By what right are you cutting down my timber, Marcion? By
whose leave are you diverting my waters, Valentinus? By what au-

thority are you moving my boundaries, Apelles? This property be-
longs to me. And all the rest of you, why are you sowing and graz-
ing here at your will? It is my property. I have been in possession
for a long time, I came into possession before you appeared. I have
good title-deeds from the original owners of the estate. I am heir
to the apostles. As they provided in their will, as they bequeathed
it in trust and confirmed it under oath, so on their terms, I hold it."
(*Prescription against Heretics,* par. 37)

The primary danger of heresy, however, is not the theft of institutions, communities, and traditions, but the corruption of the church's
proclamation. Karl Barth was adamant that the greatest enemy to the
church today is not paganism or doubt but heresy; namely, the distortion of the church's message.[19] The task of theology is to test the
proclamation of the church in the light of the Word of God in Jesus
Christ as attested in scripture. Proclamation is essential, dogmatics is
needed only for its sake.[20] "Dogmatics does not seek to give a positive, stimulating and edifying presentation. It does not even try to
give an instructive exposition in the same sense as preaching. It deals
with God, revelation and faith only in respect to their reflection in
proclamation. Even as presentation, it is also investigation and
polemic, criticism and reflection. . . . Dogmatics serves church
proclamation. . . . *"The primary task of the church is to proclaim the
Christian gospel and theology functions first of all as a test and a corrective
to measure the integrity of this proclamation."*[21] At least this has been a traditional understanding of dogmatics in Reformed theology, as clearly
stated by Karl Barth.

The church cannot be effective in its proclamation of the gospel
unless it has correctly understood the message. The first task of the
church is not to engage the world, but to get its proclamation right.
Barth understood this with great clarity. He then insisted that once
the church understood the message in the light of the revelation of
God in Jesus Christ as attested in scripture, the church was prepared
to carry on conversation with the world.[22]

Barth's emphasis is radically different from that which frequently
exists today within the church and within seminaries. Now the world
outside the church is often engaged by *the world within the church.* In
other words, the world tinctured with Christianity in the church is
carrying on conversation with the pagan world outside. Barth is a

solemn reminder that the Christian conversation must be carried on from its own foundation, that is its foundation in Jesus Christ.

Heresy is not the denial of Christian faith, but the corruption of Christian faith. The heretic is not outside but within the church.

> Heresy may take different forms. It may appear in Gnosticism as the *dilution* of Christianity by alien elements or in Marcionism as a *truncation* of the Christian faith to a mere fragment of its true self. It may result in *distortion* of the due proportion of faith even when the material from which it is constructed may lie wholly within the Christian tradition. Individual heretics may build their systems upon inconsequences of thought or language which might pass without unfavorable comment at an earlier stage of the development of doctrine, or select as a key feature a genuine Catholic datum passed beyond the limits of theological truth. To such heresies, which conserve the past without reference to the demands of the present, the term *"archaism"* may not improperly be applied. Finally, we shall see in Arianism the virtual *evacuation* of the religious content of Christianity in the interests of a barren, if coherent, metaphysic.[23]

H.E.W. Turner's analysis of heresy in the early church is surely applicable today. In recent decades, however, heresy has taken other forms. In some instances contemporary heresy is a modification of Christian faith by the legacies of Deism, the Enlightenment, and Troeltschian historicism. Contemporary theologians have, since Schleiermacher, been subject to the temptation to understand Christian faith in the light of the *dogmas* of the Enlightenment, rather than the Enlightenment in the light of the dogmas of Christian faith.

This legacy of Deism and the Enlightenment generally leads to a denial of a *personal* god who works *personally* in the created orders of history and nature, a heresy that endangers all distinctively Christian doctrines. More recently Christian theology has also been corrupted by the pressure of self-interest groups to use the language, the rhetoric, and the residual commitments of Christian faith to advance social causes and agendas.

The plight of mainline churches, so well documented in quantifiable figures, indicates that the church must once again take seriously Barth's contention that the problem today is not primarily paganism, not doubt, not the Englightenment, not the culture, but the corruptions of the Christian faith. Only when the church is clear and faithful in its exposition of the Christian faith, is it likely to have impact upon the people of contemporary society. It is documentable that the churches that have grown not only in recent decades, but also in the last several centuries have done so because they clearly proclaimed the basic fundamental Christian commitments. This has been true even when the proclamation has not been theologically sophisticated. Seminaries need to be aware that no amount of theological cleverness is ever a substitute for passionate belief in a God who is personal, who acts in history and nature, and who has acted for our salvation in Jesus Christ.

Barth's emphasis on the clear and faithful proclamation of the Christian gospel is confirmed in the history of churches. The churches that have grown and have sustained growth, clearly and openly, have proclaimed the basic Christian doctrines. It is significant today that so many of the churches in American Christianity that are growing and showing signs of vitality are those that proclaim, clearly and without equivocation, the traditional Christian convictions about God and God's work in the world.

It is significant also to note the different impact of the theology of John Wesley from the theology of Friedrich Schleiermacher on an Enlightenment society. Wesley, like Schleiermacher, was addressing persons who had been influenced by Deism, the Englightenment, and romanticism. Wesley chose to speak clearly out of the Christian tradition.[24] Schleiermacher accommodated the Christian message to the dogmas of an Enlightenment culture. The followers of Wesley, unlike the disciples of Schleiermacher, were powerful in gathering congregations, reviving churches, and even establishing a new denomination. The impact of Wesley's theology was not simply on the inner life of the church but also on the influence of the church in the world. The preachers and members of the Methodist movement were powerful in their influence in addressing the question of slavery, and the care of prisoners, as well as the care of the mentally disturbed. They played a very significant role in the modern missionary movement. Many of the leaders in the labor movement in England were lay preachers in the Methodist church. Nothing comparable has ever come out of Schleiermacherian theology.

John Wesley's way of doing theology has much to commend it today. He wrote "plain words for plain people." He did his theology out of the Bible, read as God's revelation. He mined the theological tradition, especially the early church fathers. He was not a speculative theologian, attempting to win applause by the cleverness and imagination of his mind. His writings were not political tracts attempting to give his social location in the political correctness of his day. He was content to be a "folk theologian whose intellectual competence is high, if not actually first-rate, who formulates the Christian message so that plain people may believe and live it understandingly."[25] Academic theologians during the last few decades prefer Schleiermacher to Wesley, whom they frequently ignore, but it was Wesley, not Schleiermacher, who enlarged the boundaries of the Christian faith.

Theology written in German universities and in the tradition that began with Schleiermacher fascinates many American theologians today. This theology has many striking qualities: generally a wide philosophical background, an intellectual cleverness, and not infrequently a pedantic quality. Yet those who are fascinated with this theology have not, to my knowledge, taken seriously the ineffectiveness of this theology in Germany itself and in Europe. Why has this theology so little effect on the vitality of a declining church in Europe and so little impact on social and political life? Every seminary professor needs a reality check: What do the students who have taken seriously the professor's courses accomplish when they go out as pastors? Is the theology of the university preachable so that it can sustain congregations over a period of time?

No test, defined in terms of results, can ever be final in regard to the integrity of a theology, but the capacity of certain theologies to gather congregations, nurture and sustain them, and to transform the social order and the weakness of other theologies in their inability either to establish strong communities or to sustain Christian congregations must be taken seriously.

The Test of Doctrine

Protestantism does not have a teaching office with the power to define, correct, and write doctrine. From the beginning church councils have declared certain doctrines and practices sound and others heretical. Yet there is truth in the adage that no council has ever established any Christian doctrine and no council ever destroyed any heresy.

The actions of councils were very significant as was the most significant of all councils, Nicaea. The affirmations of the Nicene Council, however, were vigorously debated in the life of the church for fifty years until they were reaffirmed at the Council of Constantinople, 381. The most reliable test of any Christian doctrine is the approbation of the people of God over a long period of time. Moreover, neither organized church nor seminary can sustain a doctrine that is not persuasive in the community of faith.

H.E.W. Turner has shrewdly commented that the best guide, though never infallible, as to Christian truth is the long-term wisdom of the Christian community. "The most important element in the evolution of Christian orthodoxy is yet to be mentioned. Behind the instinctive rejection of heresy there lay a kind of Christian common sense exercised at all its levels within the Christian church which is merely another name for the guidance of the Holy Spirit leading the church into all truth and dividing to every man severally as he wills. . . . The guidance of the Holy Spirit is never automatic. To speak of infallibility would probably be a misuse of categories."[26]

John Calvin insisted that one test of doctrine was its ability to edify. Julian N. Hartt has also argued that preachability is a criterion of good theology.[27] Certainly a decisive test of theology is its power to persuade people and to sustain communities in the Christian life. If churches and seminaries do not set boundaries, boundaries will still be set by the impotence of theologies that no longer affirm the traditional Christian gospel. An impotent theology in the seminaries means an ineffective pastor who cannot build up and lead a congregation. The congregations will wither, institutions will continue to decay, and finally endowments raised by other hands may deteriorate. In theology as in every human enterprise there is a judgment, but the judgment is sometimes slow in coming. Finally, congregations will set boundaries, if church governing bodies and seminaries do not.

3

Teaching the Church's Faith

The first task of the seminary is to teach the church's faith; more particularly, a Presbyterian seminary is to teach the faith of the Presbyterian Church. A generation ago, up until the 1950s, this was taken for granted in Presbyterian seminaries. It can now no longer be taken for granted.

As seminaries have lost their identity as church institutions and have become freestanding institutions for theological thought and reflection, they have lost their sharp focus.

The Problem

The reasons for this loss of focus are at least threefold. First, the prevalent conviction that the faith the church has confessed in the past is not adequate for a post-Enlightenment culture, the idea that faith must be accommodated to culture has undermined the teaching of the church's faith.

The times, it is believed, call for a new understanding of faith. Friedrich Schleiermacher (1768–1834), who understood the challenge of the Enlightenment and gave his life to writing a theology that took the Enlightenment seriously but also that sought to maintain the faith, is the source of much of the new theology that was to come. No one can doubt Schleiermacher's brilliance or even his intention to be Christian. Yet it is possible and must be asked, if he did

not indeed give away too much in accommodating the Enlightenment and Romantic cultures. Can Christian faith be Christian faith
without the Old and New Testaments as the written Word of God,
without a personal God who works personally in the created orders
of history and nature, without a doctrine of eternal life worth believing? In any case, Schleiermacher does not belong to the tradition that
built the Presbyterian Church in this country. Yet in recent years the
theological influence of Schleiermacher and the tradition of theology
that roots in him have penetrated Presbyterian seminaries. The conviction that the old faith is not good enough for today is combined
with the hubris of theologians that leaves them uncontent to master
and interpret the tradition and that produces the abundance of theologies that seek to be creative solutions of theological problems. These
new theologies, it is thought, will serve better than the great theologies of the past but none of them has been persuasive to modern people in general and to congregations in particular.

Theology becomes self-destructive when its primary goal is ac-
commodation to the culture. This has been well illustrated in the history of theology in America. James Turner, in his book *Without God,
Without Creed,* has documented how an overzealous effort to accommodate the culture outside the circle of faith actually contributed in
America to the rise of unbelief.

> The crucial ingredient, then, in the mix that produced an endur-
> ing unbelief was the choices of believers. More precisely, unbelief
> resulted from the decisions that influential church leaders—lay
> writers, theologians, ministers—made about how to confront the
> modern pressures upon religious belief. Not all of their selections
> resulted from long thought and careful reflection; part of our hu-
> manity, after all, is that we have much in common with lemmings.
> But they were choices. And the choices, taken together, boiled
> down to a decision to deal with modernity by embracing it—to
> defuse modern threats to the traditional bases of belief by bringing
> God into line with modernity.
>
> In tailoring belief more closely to human understanding and
> aspiration, however, many religious leaders made a fatal slip.
> They were not wrong to think that any significant faith would
> have to express itself in moral practice. But they often forgot that
> their God's purposes were not supposed to be man's. They were
> not mistaken in believing that any resilient belief must ground

itself in human thought and experience. But they frequently forgot the tension that, by definition, must exist between an incomprehensible God and the human effort to know Him. They were hardly fools to insist that any God must be lord of this world, but they did not always remember that this world could not define Him. They forgot, in short, that their God was as any God had to be to command belief over the long term—radically other than man.

Put slightly differently, unbelief emerged because church leaders too often forgot the transcendence essential to any worthwhile God. They committed religion *functionally* to making the world better in human terms and *intellectually* to modes of knowing God fitted only for understanding this world.[1]

Karl Barth rightly observed, I think, that Christian believers do not face today any temptations to doubt or unbelief that they have not always faced. The peculiarities of our age ought not to be an excuse for our failures to proclaim the gospel as Christians have believed and confessed it through the centuries.

The second reason for the loss of focus is the seminary's embrace of a multitude of causes. These causes range from an obsession with various forms of self-perceived oppression to such issues as abortion and the environment. Subject matter that was once covered in courses in church history or in doctrine have now become major items in the curriculum, ranging from spirituality, to worship, to marriage, to conflict management. The cause orientation of seminary campuses not only takes time from the study of basic texts, but it also changes the focus of the seminary from its primary tasks of educating ministers to preach the gospel of what God has done and is doing for human beings to the advocacy of "causes" that are flawed and that will die.

A cause-oriented seminary campus not only exploits the gospel of what God has done for our salvation but also the theological enterprise itself for ideological purposes. The use of the gospel and theology itself to justify parochial, flawed causes from education to economic and political platforms, to intricate foreign policy decisions, to the advancements of the causes of particular groups corrupts the theological and teaching task of the seminary. The result is loss of respect and authority as well as the ability to educate pastors who can nurture and build congregations.

Catechetical Instruction
or Graduate School

A third reason for the confusion in the focus of the seminary on teaching the church's faith is the increasing tendency to turn the seminary into a graduate school or to assume the functions of a secular university. The problem can be put in another way. Is the seminary a catechetical institution or is it a graduate institution for critical study of religion? These options are not necessarily exclusive, but it is critically important for the church that they are put together in such a way that the life of a theological institution whose purpose is to train pastors is not undermined.

Seminaries increasingly in our time aspire to be centers for advanced religious studies. Critical reflection on the faith, rather than proclaiming and transmitting the faith, becomes the primary focus. This change in the direction of the seminary harmonizes with the increasing self-image of the faculty as scholars rather than teachers of the faith. In the modern seminary research, articles for review, the writing of books, and attendance at professional organizations have a role for faculty that they did not have even for faculties in university divinity schools fifty years ago.

The contemporary model of the seminary as an institution for advanced study presupposes that seminary students have finished catechetical training. This assumption may have been partially true fifty years ago when many theological students had completed two yearlong college courses in Bible content and many had read New Testament Greek before matriculating in the seminary. Furthermore, in the South a considerable number of seminary students as late as the 1940s had recited the Shorter Catechism. In 1923, more than 14,000 southern Presbyterians recited the Catechism, reporting their achievement to the Presbyterian Committee on Publications, receiving Bibles and certificates from an appreciative church and having their names printed in the annual honor roll in the *Christian Observer*. Some of them came to the seminary. Yet even then, most students had not really finished catechetical instruction. Today, students come to the seminary not only without training in any biblical language or catechism or Bible, but also with a great variety of degrees, ranging from engineering to art. It can no longer be assumed that the seminary student is a graduate in the humanities with major study in such fields as

English, history, and philosophy. Seminaries for the most part have given up any effort to have remedial courses for these deficiencies in college training. The simple fact is that the students who come to the theological seminary today have not finished catechetical training. They cannot go beyond catechetical training until they do.

The contemporary model also presupposes that faculties have completed catechetical training. This is an unwise assumption. Ph.D. degrees can be earned in specific religious fields without any major study in the Bible or church history or doctrine, depending on the field of concentration. A seminary degree is no longer a requirement for seminary teaching.

Seminaries cannot assume anymore that students and sometime faculty arrive knowing the church's faith or that they are prepared for critical reflection. The result is that ministers are sent out into the church frequently with no knowledge in depth of the church's faith. This is the crisis in theological education.

The Content of the Faith

The renewal of the seminaries must begin with the teaching of the *church's* faith. What is the *content* of this faith? The traditional Presbyterian answer is clear: the Bible and a coherent, comprehensive statement of the faith as found in the official confessions and systematic theologies that through long use have received the approbation of the Presbyterian community.

Doctrine,
as the Church's Faith

Contemporary seminaries have more than a sufficient number of courses in Bible and theology. Yet they do not always meet the requirement of teaching the church's faith. Sharply focused technical courses, however competent, do not give the student a comprehensive knowledge of the scriptures as God's Word. Learned courses on theological issues and problems do not give a student a coherent, comprehensive knowledge of Christian faith or a vision of the reality of the orders of nature and history in the light of that faith, what Otto Weber called a ground plan of the created order.

In an earlier day, seminaries frequently devoted an entire year to the mastery of Reformed theology. Until World War II, these courses focused on the mastery of a text that had received approbation in the church. Charles Hodge's *Systematic Theology* was the most widely used text in the late nineteenth century. Other similar texts summarized the Christian faith from a Reformed perspective: the theologies of William Shedd (1820–1894), Henry B. Smith (1815–1877), A. Strong (1836–1921), and Robert Dabney (1820–1898). Heinrich L. Heppe's (1820–1879) *Reformed Dogmatics* served the same role in Europe, and, when it was translated, in the United States. In the early 1940s, Louis Berkhof's *Systematic Theology* was widely used in Presbyterian seminaries. In the 1940s and 1950s, Emil Brunner's *Dogmatics* (1946–1960) was sometimes taught.

It is possible to be critical and even caustic in the criticism of this method of teaching from one or a few texts. Yet the old method ought not to be dismissed. These texts were comprehensive statements of Christian faith from a particular church's perspective. They were written so they could be easily mastered with paragraph headings as well as chapter headings. They covered the whole range of theology and ethics from creation to the consummation. A student of average gifts could graduate from the seminary having a comprehensive understanding of what had been an approved statement of Reformed faith.

Comprehensive, coherent but relatively brief summaries of the faith have always been an important means of teaching and transmitting the faith. These statements grew out of the life of the church and had the approbation of the people. They provided a framework of interpretation that enabled the reader to comprehend human existence in the light of the revelation of God in Jesus Christ, beginning with the creation and ending with the consummation of all things. They included all the major Christian affirmations. They provided in brief compass a comprehensive, coherent statement of faith that the ordinary Christian could understand.[2]

These statements go back to the ancient rules of faith and include such writings as Irenaeus, *Demonstration of the Apostolic Preaching, Against Heresies*; Augustine, *Enchiridion*; Calvin, *Institutes of the Christian Religion*; Reformed confessions; William Ames, *Marrow of Divinity*; A. A. Hodge, *Outlines of Theology*. Karl Barth, the greatest Reformed theologian of the twentieth century, provided a remarkable thirteen-volume *Church Dogmatics* (unfinished at his death). It is a great loss that he did not provide a one-volume summary that ordinary seminary students could master.

The plethora of theologies now current in seminaries and in the life of the church leave ministers and church members with no clear sense of identity and no comprehensive framework of theology in the context of which they can understand the world and their own lives.

In contemporary seminaries there is seldom the effort to master one particular text. There are various reasons for this; no one text has the universal approval that Hodge's theology had in American Presbyterianism in the nineteenth century and the first half of the twentieth century. Today there is a pervasive tendency for professors of theology to teach their own understanding of Christian faith, using a whole variety of textbooks. The result is that seminary students graduate, having read a few pages from Tillich, a few pages from Barth, a few pages from the various theologians from the second half of the twentieth century, but without mastering any comprehensive statement of Christian faith and frequently without covering many specific doctrines in detail.

The loss of a comprehensive statement of Christian faith that has received the approbation of the church and that has demonstrated the power to gather congregations and build congregations is further complicated by the decline in courses in the history of Christian doctrine, such as those taught by Robert L. Calhoun at Yale University and taught with less brilliance by professors in many other theological institutions. The teaching of courses in the history of Christian doctrine was predicated on the conviction that one needed to know how the church had understood the faith in the preceding centuries in order to state the faith in the contemporary world. Yet this understanding of theology and of the importance of the history of doctrine for theological work today was not shared by many theologians after 1955. A professor of the history of Christian doctrine who taught in a very prestigious university told me that he was called to that position, not because history of doctrine was thought to be necessary for theological education or for theology today, but for tradition's sake. In my own situation at Union Theological Seminary there was continual pressure after my first several years there to reduce the time for the history of Christian doctrine or to seek to eliminate it.

Three reasons account for the decline in courses in history of doctrine. First, the field is so vast that no one person can master it. Second, many contemporary theologians do not appear to regard the history of the church's reflection on the faith as necessary for theological reflection today. The third reason is academic pettiness. Historians claim that the history of doctrine is covered in their classes, though to my knowledge it never is. The situation can be reversed, as it was at Columbia Theological Seminary when the theologians opposed the excellent course on the history of doctrine taught in the history department by William C. Robinson. It is worth noting that at Yale Divinity School in the 1940s a magnificent course in the history of Christianity, taught by Roland Bainton, and one of the most effective courses in the history of doctrine to be found anywhere, taught by Robert C. Calhoun, existed in the same curriculum without any jealousy that I as a student observed. For whatever reason, the decline of the study of the history of doctrine is a great loss to theological education and the church.

The crisis in the seminaries is that they no longer assume the primary responsibility for teaching the *church's* faith, which includes the history of Christian doctrine and a comprehensive statement of Christian faith that has received the approbation of the people of God and has demonstrated power to edify and to build up congregations.

Scripture Read as the Word of God, and as the Interpretative Context for Understanding Human Existence in the World

The foundation of the church's faith is the scripture. The scripture according to the Presbyterian tradition is the Word of God written. As such, it is the final authority for life in the church, not simply for the life of the people among whom it was written. The scriptures provided a witness to revelation, and by the power of the Holy Spirit they become revelation themselves. They also provided the language for the faith.

Scripture read as revelation or as the narrative of God's dealing with his creation provides two indispensable foundations for the study of theology and preparation for the ministry. The first is the interpretative framework for understanding human existence. The Bible begins with God's creation of the world, and it ends with the consummation of all things. In between is the promise to Abraham, the deliverance from Pharaoh's bondage and the giving of the law,

the Davidic kingdom, the prophets, culminating in the fulfillment of
the promises in Jesus Christ. The biblical narrative discloses a God
who is both Lord and Redeemer and who works in the created orders of nature and history.

This comprehensive grasp of the scripture—namely, the narrative
of God's work in creation, providence, and redemption and the narrative of the human story from Adam and his fall, the call of Abraham, Moses and the exodus, David, the prophets, and the fulfillment
of this history in the life and death of Jesus Christ, whom God raised
from the dead, the apostles, and the consummation of all things in a
new heaven and new earth—established the authority of scripture
over theology. Exegesis of particular texts and the theology of biblical books have to fit into this biblical frame of reference. Scripture, as
the Westminster Confession puts it, is interpreted by scripture. Every
authentic Christian theological affirmation must be biblical in the
sense of fitting into this interpretative framework.

This comprehensive knowledge of scripture also corrected and
shaped the theology of church members who were untrained in theology but were nevertheless very good theologians, more to be
trusted at times than seminary professors. Unfortunately secular education, the secularity of the elite media, and the failure of teaching in
churches have undermined this biblical knowledge that identified the
Christian community. Yet this comprehensive biblical understanding
of human history is easily accessible to any literate person who reads
the English Bible, especially if read devotionally in the context of the
church. A prerequisite for any candidate for the ministry ought to be,
as I have suggested to presbytery committees, reading the Bible
through from Genesis to Revelation. Certainly seminaries should
make this biblical knowledge, which ought to be in the possession of
every Christian, a prerequisite for serious theological studies.

Fifty years ago this vision of reality was endemic in our culture.
Those who did not read the Bible learned it from the culture, from
ordinary conversation, and from schools. Most church colleges required courses in the *content* of the Old and New Testaments. In addition, many read the Bible themselves in regular devotions and in
programs sponsored by the church and the American Bible Society.

Today the scriptural vision of reality is increasingly lost. Many students come to the seminary without having college courses in the
content of the Old and New Testaments and without the study of

biblical texts in church school and family devotions. Some do not know John 3:16. Lacking this interpretative framework, they are easily pushed about by every wind of doctrine.

The second great service this biblical awareness provides the education of ministers is a common language and a language coherent with the content of the faith itself. The really great theologies that have built and nurtured Christian communities have almost without exception been expressed in biblical language.[3]

The English-speaking world is fortunate that the English language was shaped in very considerable measure by people who were engaged in the translating of the Bible and wanted a language that was adequate to convey the biblical content.[4] We owe very much in contemporary English to translators such as William Tyndale, to the translators of the King James Version of the Bible, as well as to William Shakespeare. The English language is now being shaped by many other forces, but in its origin it was in part created by an effort to have an adequate language to state Christian faith.

English-speaking Christians have profited greatly by an English translation of the Bible, founded in work of Tyndale, that in remarkable ways expresses the faith of the ancient scriptures. Moreover, this language was spoken by everyone. The language of the scripture was the language that was very familiar to church people and not only to church people but to society. We increasingly face a situation in the life of the church in which people do not speak the language of Christian faith. This language becomes a foreign tongue because the language of the public school and the university is increasingly shaped by secular forces.

The Bible not only gave us language, but it also gave us the narratives and stories of the faith. It gave us the witness to the revelation of God in Jesus Christ. There cannot be a Presbyterian church, there cannot be a Protestant church, without knowledge of the Bible in depth so that the language of scripture is the "native" tongue of the Christian.

The recovery of the reading of the Bible as scripture, not as a piece of Near Eastern literature and not as a text for scientific study, must have priority in the seminary. The seminary must maintain the historical and scientific integrity of the study of scripture, but this must be done in the context of the church's faith and commitment. The scientific study of scripture must *presuppose* a prior, comprehensive, and deeply personal knowledge of scripture.

The first task of the theological seminary is to assure people in the church that its graduates have read the Bible and know the Bible in English. Fifty years ago seminaries had courses in English Bible. These were later supplanted by courses in the Greek New Testament which are far more limited in scope than courses that required the reading of the whole of the scriptures. One of the great achievements of Protestant Christianity is not only the translation of the Bible but also the critical study of scripture. Yet highly technical courses in scripture cannot substitute for the comprehensive reading of the scripture or the devotional reading of scripture.

The effectiveness of technical, critical historical studies of the Bible in the preparation of pastors presupposes the narrative reading of scripture as the acts of God for human salvation.

The agenda and context for the study of scripture must be set by the faith of the worshiping, believing community that built seminaries to prepare pastors. The questions Christians ask of their scriptures differ significantly from those of secular scholarship. The questions that critical historical studies ask are not the most important questions. They are not the questions that make the scriptures worth studying. The importance of the study of the Bible in the context of faith has been well stated in a recent book on biblical theology.

> The underlying question here is the relationship between theology and secular biblical scholarship. The solution that dispenses with a genuinely theological Old and New Testament theology implies that theologians should follow the fluctuations of biblical scholarship, but not seek to influence their direction.
>
> That is a dangerous policy for theologians to pursue in a culture where the subject-matter of the Bible is contested. Historians and believers may read it very differently. The real justification for letting biblical scholarship set the agenda for theological interpretation of the Bible is that the scholars' questions are those of the contemporary culture which theology seeks to address. But that is only part of the truth. The world may have more to learn from the Bible than what the scholars are experts in unraveling. A theology (and so a theological interpretation of the Bible) which allowed itself to be directed by the discoveries of biblical scholarship alone would be starved of fresh air and suffocate. Believers have other interests in the Bible, and there is no reason why these too should not guide and motivate (though not compel) their biblical interpretation. These other interests may also draw upon the resources of

scholarship. . . . Historical scholarship has its own agenda and its own secular university base, even if its numerical strength remains parasitic upon people's religious interests in these texts.[5]

The importance of reading the Bible not as another book, such as Homer's *Odyssey,* but as the narrative of the acts of the triune God and God's struggle with his people has been well stated by George Lindbeck. He further argued for the priority of the narrative meaning of scripture since critical historical studies of the Bible asked a different set of questions.

Instead of asking what the biblical narratives tell about God and human beings, or how they are to be used in shaping life and understanding reality, the primary question became whether they are accurate reports of the events of which they tell. The narrative meaning of the stories was confused with their factual (scientific and historical) meaning, and was thereby lost.

Not everyone remained interested in factual meaning, as we shall note in a moment, but those who did divided into two camps: inerrantists and historical critics. Both tended to think that facts (defined by the prevailing rational and empirical standards of the day) are what are important in any document, and most notably in the book of books, the Bible. Their disagreement was over the factual veracity of the text or, more broadly, over how to go about determining the factual meaning. The inerrantist tendency was to insist that everything which could by any stretch of the imagination be supposed to be a factual assertion must be so interpreted and accepted as accurate; while historical critics used the text as a source of data for reconstructing what could (by the general, and never entirely stable, standards of the day) be plausibly taken to be the originating events, personalities, or situations (e.g., the historical Jesus). There were many gradations between the extremes, but for all the participants in the debate, from fundamentalist rigorists to hyperskeptical liberals, the narrative meaning had collapsed into the factual and disappeared.[6]

Critical historical study and the secular university are never faith neutral. The faith commitments of the scholar always inform the works of the scholar. The scholar studying the Bible may not only be hostile to the Bible as the Word of God, but also bitterly anti-church.

While affirming the necessity of historical criticism and even the presence of secular historical-critical scholars to keep their religious colleagues honest, Jon Levenson insists that historical critics must be challenged to make public their own motivations and assumptions. The axioms of Troeltschian historicism are prior commitments. Historicism cannot "exempt itself from its own verdict about all human thought."[7]

The human self has been endowed with powers of transcendence that give the self some freedom in assessing data over pre-understandings, faith commitments, and biases. Yet this freedom is never complete and hence claims of a truly objective study of scripture or any other text should be questioned, as for example the claims made by spokesmen for the Jesus Seminar.[8]

The faith factor that informs all understanding must be taken with great seriousness by theological seminaries, especially in the study of scripture. The Bible must be taught in seminaries so that students come under the power of the Holy Spirit to cherish it as God's Word to each Christian believer and to the Christian community. Professors cannot do the work of the Holy Spirit, but they ought not create difficulties for the work of the Holy Spirit, much less a defiance of the Holy Spirit. Scholarship alone, much less political correctness, does not qualify anyone to teach in a seminary.

Honorable people believe that the Bible, however interesting, is just another piece of Near Eastern literature. But no honorable person can teach biblical studies in a seminary without cherishing the Bible as God's holy word for all people.

The crisis in the seminary is the refusal of contemporary theological institutions to take seriously the teaching of the faith, which, first of all, means teaching the people what is in the written text of the scriptures. Critical reflection on the scriptures can come only after students have read the Bible as members of the Christian community and in the light of the church's faith.

The crisis is also the failure of seminaries to teach a comprehensive statement of Christian faith that has received the approbation of the Christian community and, in particular, of the Presbyterian Church.

Christopher Seitz of Yale Divinity School has stated the teaching task of the church with great clarity and great precision:

> What are the implications of this biblical understanding of revelation and pluralism for Christians today? Stripped to essentials, Christian ministry begins with the capacity to make a robust, intelligent accounting of the faith we hold. Can we state with clarity

and conviction what it is that we believe, as this has been handed
down to us? What does it mean to say that we worship a crucified
and risen Lord? That we believe in a final judgment of the quick
and the dead? That we believe the God who created the world is
not identical with creation? That we look to Christ's return in
glory? Before we move to commend the faith to others in this pluralistic society—however we might do that—can we first state
with comprehensiveness and conviction what it is that we ourselves believe, as this has been handed down to us, from Israel to
the apostles and from one generation of faith to the next?

So before we run to tackle some agreed-upon benevolent activity, before we defer to the wisdom of the age because it has the
imprimatur of the talk-show hosts, before we assume that ministry
involves others more inspired or more suited or more whatever
than ourselves, it should not be forgotten that ministry begins with
the simple confession of faith corporately held. The church is the
place where that faith is taught, preached, nurtured, and shared.
The world is where that faith is passed on with vigor, humor, and
compassion.[9]

Teaching the Church's Faith
vs. Constructive Theology

Constructive Theology has been a great emphasis in theological
education since the 1950s. Theologian after theologian has sought to
write the new theology that would persuade modern people. A par-
tial list of these new theologies would include The New Quest for
the Historical Jesus, Linguistic Analysis, The Theology of the Secular, Jesus Theology, Theology as Literature, Death of God Theology,
Game Theology, The Greening of America and Consciousness III,
The Theology of Hope, The Communist-Christian Dialogue, The
Theology of Play, Black Theology, Liberation Theology, Feminist
Theology.

Most of these theologies were written out of the conviction that
the new Reformation theologies of Brunner and Barth had not fully
investigated certain questions that the Enlightenment had raised and
that they were not sufficiently concerned about the transformation of
society. They also arose out of particular concerns of the 1960s and
1970s. The new theologians all had in common the intent to write a
theology that would persuade modern people. Yet the most significant

characteristic of these new theologies, either in the United States or in Europe, has been an inability to persuade modern people. None has demonstrated a power to gather congregations and build them up to maturity. The lifetime of these new theologies has been very brief, except in the case of black theology and feminist theology that articulated the cause and interest of particular groups.

The plethora of theologies in the last fifty years has contributed to a *break* with the past. All the contemporary theologies have been more concerned with answering the questions of the present than with articulating the theological heritage. Hence, it is very difficult to relate theologies of the last fifty years as well as many of the new theologies of the nineteenth century to older traditions. The focus was not on the tradition but on the contemporary situation. This led to a loss of rootage and depth that comes with the tradition. The new theologies were in considerable measure a product of the world within the church, rather than a dialogue out of the church's traditional faith with the world.

The great variety of contemporary theologies has contributed not only to a break with the past but also to the loss of a common theological language. Albert Outler once noted that many contemporary theologies were characterized by lust for novelty and a narcissistic delight in being different. In many cases they have formulated a new vocabulary. This contributed to a loss of the theological vocabulary that had become universal in Presbyterian churches from the sixteenth century until World War II. The Presbyterian churches fifty years ago spoke the same theological vocabulary in church school, in preaching, and in theological seminary. This common theological language had been hammered out by Reformed theology in the seventeenth century and was a remarkable achievement. This has now been lost.

The seminaries have done very little to provide a common language for the churches. An equally serious source of the problem with language is not only biblical illiteracy, but the incredible diversity in teaching Christian doctrine in Presbyterian seminaries. The diversity is the consequence of the seminary's lost sense of responsibility to teach the *church's* theology. The increasing tendency for theologians in the last thirty years, to attempt to write a new theology, not only failed in writing a persuasive theology, but it also succeeded in breaking down the theological consensus and the theological language that had been a strength of the church.

Albert Outler, a great teacher of the past generation, always insisted that the theological enterprise should beware of hubris, and emphasize modesty. The theologian should aspire to be an adequate interpreter of the tradition and to articulate it effectively in his or her particular time and place. If in the process of this *modest* enterprise of understanding and articulating a tradition, something more happens, well and good. The desire to write the creative new theology may in itself be self-defeating. Creative theologians are very few in the history of the church.

The great theologies have come out of the modest intentions to state the faith of the church with integrity and clarity. Any "new" theology confessed the old theology in content and language. Any changes were modest and congruent with what had gone before. The law of minimal theological development was widely observed in times past. It guided the theological work of the great theologians of the fourth and fifth centuries. The theologians of Nicaea and Chalcedon wanted to say as little as possible that was new. They wanted to answer the questions of the new generation with what the church had already approved. Only when it was absolutely necessary to refute heresies and to correct aberrations in the faith, did they add phrases to the creed or to their theological text. The same was true with John Calvin. He modestly attempted to proclaim the theology of scripture and the church and to say as little new as was possible.

Creative theologies have been very few in the history of the church. Not many are chosen to be the creative theologians who write the great textbooks or the great summaries of faith. The very fact that creative theologies have been so few in the past should restrain the ambition of theologians to write new theologies in our time. It is much safer, both the for theologian and for the church, to master the theology that has received the approbation of the church and that has been productive in the gathering of congregations. The continual publication of new theologies that have been powerless to gather congregations, to build up church attendance, and to vitalize the church has not been very useful in the education of ministers.

Ernst Benz (1907–), a liberal theologian of the past generation, once observed that theologians should tell the truth.[10] They should not use the words of Christian faith to cover up their denial of basic Christian doctrines. They should not deceive Christian believers. The denial of a personal God and of the incarnation and the resurrection should not be hidden behind clever phrases and traditional Christian words. In some instances theologians may be seeking a way to still be Christian when they can no longer affirm basic doctrines of the Christian tradition, but this should be honestly stated. The theologian must be respected in the struggle for faith. The right to teach on a seminary faculty, however, must be challenged for a theologian, who can no longer affirm or intends to affirm in heart and mind basic Christian doctrines. Seminary professors must be beyond the struggle of wondering if a Christian theology is possible.

E. L. Mascall has made an acute observation that much contemporary theology is both sophisticated and naive. It is sophisticated in that only a clever person could have written it. It is naive in that no "ordinary person . . . could think Christianity was worth practicing if they thought this position to be true," that is, if that person understood what the theologian was saying.[11]

The Problem of "Distance"
and Perspective

Teaching the faith does not mean indoctrination. It does not mean the loss of critical judgment. Faith is not credulity. The Augustinian dictum "We believe in order to understand" emphasizes the critical role of reason. Without reason we cannot believe, and without reason we cannot distinguish faith from credulity, as Augustine well knew. Reason is not the monopoly of the secular university.

The proper teaching of the church's faith has its own built-in safeguards against indoctrination and credulity. First of all, the seminary in teaching the church's faith acknowledges that it teaches this faith out of a particular tradition. In the broad context this is the tradition of Western culture that includes the contributions of Greek philosophy and of Roman society.

Theology in the Western world has been expressed in the language that was shaped by Greek philosophy and by the literature of ancient cultures as well as the particular history of Western Europe. Many today deplore the particularity of Western theology. It should be acknowledged that this is only one way of stating Christian faith. Yet there should also be gratitude that the language of Greek philosophy as well as the great literature of the ancient world have proved so effective a vehicle for stating Christian faith. For this we should be grateful. The fact that the church acknowledges that it speaks out of one particular tradition enables it to bring critical judgment to the task of theology.

The church in teaching its faith acknowledges that it not only uses a particular tradition to articulate theology but that its theology is based on a *particular* revelation of God in the history of Israel, from the call of Abraham and to the culmination in the life, death, and resurrection of Jesus Christ and the giving of the Holy Spirit. The church's best theology has never obscured the particularity of its foundation. This self-acknowledgment provides a basis for critical judgment.

The church's teaching has a second safeguard. The primary task of theology, as Karl Barth emphasized, is to maintain the integrity of Christian theology. In Christian theology the church's proclamation is tested for its faithfulness to the Revelation which is its foundation. The task of theology is critical examination and reflection on that faith as to its integrity and faithfulness.

The teaching of the church's faith has a third safeguard. Teaching is not simply repetition of past formulas but the exposition of the faith in a way that makes sense out of human life and community. An exposition of the faith that does not illuminate and make sense out of experience, especially experience in the Christian community, cannot long endure. Christian theology that endures must finally make more sense out of the stubborn realities of life than any other faith. Every faith must face what William James called "the gauntlet of confrontation with the total context of experience." In addition, the consequences of any faith are seen in the lives it shapes and the societies it informs. For this reason, simple indoctrination cannot long endure.

Teaching the faith is no dull and uncritical exercise. It has the safeguards of (1) acknowledging its own tradition, (2) testing the integrity of its own proclamation, (3) making sense out of contemporary life and experience, and (4) meeting the test of faith in the formation of persons and communities.

The human spirit has the remarkable capacity to objectify its own self-existence. And therefore, human beings can critically reflect on culture, on personal history, and on the various biochemical urges that motivate life. In a similar manner the Christian believer standing in a particular tradition can objectify and pass judgment on its integrity and its capacity to illuminate life and make sense out of human experience. In this way, the teaching of faith in a theological seminary can provide "distance" and critical judgment.

Furthermore, the theological seminary's teaching the church's faith is not wholly different from teaching and research in the university. In the university knowledge is not communicated and research is not carried on apart from a variety of traditions and faith commitments, sometimes unacknowledged. The university can be safe only as it too engages in critical self-reflection.

The Problem of Graduate Education

The purposes of a graduate school and of a seminary are different. The seminaries have as their purpose the preparation of pastors. The graduate school's purpose is to educate scholars who teach and who do research. The significance of preparation for the ministry for the church is obvious. The preparation of scholars who can teach and do research is also of significance for the church.

Yale University began giving Ph.D.'s in 1861 following the German practice. In the 1870s the University of Pennsylvania and Harvard, Columbia, and Princeton universities in that order also began to offer programs leading to the Ph.D. degree, and the University of Chicago, founded in 1891, made the degree "the pinnacle of the academic program."[12] By the time of World War II the Ph.D. had become the standard preparation for teaching, though many of the ablest teachers in seminaries and in colleges at that time did not have Ph.D.'s or any other graduate training. After World War II the Doctor of Philosophy degree had become the basic requirement for membership on a college or seminary faculty.

The establishment of the Ph.D. as a basic requirement for teaching led to a great expansion of Ph.D. programs. Fifty years ago only the ablest students in their classes could be admitted to Ph.D. programs and only a few major universities undertook graduate training. All of this was changed with the demand for Ph.D.'s. Programs granting doctorates became prolific in state and private institutions. The Ph.D. has remained the standard requirement for teaching, but the holding of a degree does not guarantee the competence that it once did.

Moreover, the tremendous expansion of graduate programs has led to an excess of Ph.D.'s in many fields. This is especially true for white males in theological disciplines.

The Doctor of Philosophy programs, for all the inflation of the value of the degree in recent years, have added competence to theological education. For the foreseeable future they will continue to be indispensable. Yet the Ph.D. program is not the solution to all problems.

Many great seminary teachers as late as the 1950s, it is important to remember, did not have the Ph.D. degree or even graduate study. My first course in theology was taught by a very able professor, G. G. Parkinson of Erskine College and Seminary, Due West, South Carolina, who had never done graduate work. He used as his basic text the systematic theologies of Charles Hodge and of Louis Berkhof. I can give my testimony that no one I know today teaches the church's faith more effectively to students preparing for the ministry.

The calling of ministers with significant achievement in the pastorate to be professors does not appear to have a promising future. The nature of the pastorate today and the ethos of the church have not encouraged ministers in serious and systematic study and in developing personal theological strength and a capacity for self-determination and critical thinking. Few experiences are sadder than to bring a pastor, who once had promising gifts to be a scholar, to be a teacher in the seminary and then to discover that he has been so long away from serious study that he can no longer read a serious book or engage in theological discussion of any great depth. The ablest graduates of the seminary where I taught for thirty-one years are overwhelmingly in the pastorate. Yet the pastorate today and the pressures in the church do not encourage pastors in general to maintain their theological skills and abilities.

Seminaries can call younger pastors with great academic abilities and also with authentic experience in the pastorate and then have them go to graduate schools in preparation for teaching. This route was once chosen by at least two southern Presbyterian seminaries. The abundance of Ph.D.'s looking for teaching positions removes the pressure for the seminary to engage in this kind of call, even though this method of calling a professor could increase the competence of faculty to educate pastors.

The church may face an acute dilemma in the future in the calling of teachers. The pressure will be increasingly to take the easiest route and to call theological seminary teachers from a pool of graduate school Ph.D.'s, many of whom have had their training in increasingly secular universities.

At this point my own personal recollection of my decisions as a young seminarian may be appropriate. President J. McDowell Richards of Columbia Theological Seminary asked me during my senior year what I would like to do in the life of the church if I could simply choose my own future. I told him without a moment's hesitation I would like either to be pastor of the Presbyterian church at Chapel Hill, North Carolina, or to teach in a seminary. My life came very close to fulfilling those two intentions.

I knew as a senior in a seminary that graduate study was important, crucial if I were to teach and very helpful if I were to be the kind of Presbyterian pastor I intended. Dean John Keith Benton of the Vanderbilt University School of Religion told me that there was only one graduate school that would really fulfill my intentions and that was Yale of that era 1946–1948. At Yale the professors who had primary responsibility for my graduate education were Albert Outler, Roland Bainton, Robert L. Calhoun, and Kenneth Scott Latourette, who was in charge of the Graduate Studies Program. Each of my graduate school teachers was a devout Christian. Some had commitments to particular causes, for example, Roland Bainton and the cause of peace. Yet graduate study at Yale was not ideological. It concentrated on the mastery of data, as well as critical theological reflection. Three of the professors who taught me at Yale would later preach in the church of which I was pastor. I do not know of any faculty today that matches that faculty at Yale of that era in intellectual competence and in Christian commitment. Professor Calhoun, when I was a graduate student, was known as a liberal with bloodied but unbowed head. Yet in the perspective of today Robert Calhoun was, as Hans Frei noted in a memorial address, conservative in theology.

It is also important to note that when I was a graduate student at Yale, Battell Chapel was openly acknowledged as the Christian community on the Yale University campus and President Charles Seymour frequently read the scripture.[13] With the radical secularization of major universities the kind of graduate training in theology that I received at Yale is less and less a possibility.

The church must give attention to the long-range consequences of choosing so many of its teachers out of Ph.D. applicants who have received their graduate training in secular universities, who are the graduates of a relatively few universities, and who fellowship together in professional organizations that are frequently secular or are driven by the current theological pressures. The relatively small number of graduate schools that provide seminary teachers and the peer pressure of organizations means that the teachers of the church increasingly belong to their own community whose purposes are not always the purposes of the church. No one can predict now how these problems will work themselves out in the future, but it is clear enough that the source of the church's teachers is a matter to which the church itself must increasingly give its attention.

4

Teaching
Church Practice

Seminary teaching has always been concerned with church practice. The pastor not only thinks but does. The work of the Protestant pastor, the Reformed and Presbyterian pastor in particular,
has been radically different from the medieval priest. The Protestant pastor has the same status and power as any Christian. The pastor cannot in
principle do anything a Christian, as such, cannot do for himself or her-
self. The pastor differs from other Christians only in competence to interpret, preach, and teach the scriptures. As such the pastor performs
critically important functions in the church. Practice, not power or status, is crucial for the Presbyterian pastor. Protestants have pastors only so
that important works, essential to the life of the believing congregations,
can be done with competency, decency, and order.

Church practice has always been critically important for Reformed
Christians. It was crucially important for Calvin. His letters are pastoral.[1]
He understood his primary calling in Geneva, not as a theologian, but
as a pastor. The first task to which he put his hand on returning to
Geneva in 1541 was writing a polity that included such pastoral prac-
tices as teaching, visitation, and the discipline of the congregation.

Martin Bucer (1491–1551), the Reformer in Strasbourg to whom
Calvin was indebted, realized in the beginning that the Reformed
church had to devise new methods of nurturing people in the faith. He
devoted an entire book to pastoral care. He pioneered in the use of catechetical training and admission to the Lord's Table as a means not only
of teaching the faith, but of developing the life of the community.[2]

Bucer's definition of pastoral care is still valid, "To draw to Christ those who are alienated; to lead back those who have been drawn away; to secure amendment of life in those who fall into sin; to strengthen weak and sickly Christians; to preserve Christians who are whole and strong, and urge them forward in all good."[3]

The Reformed Pastor by Richard Baxter (1651–1691) stands with Bucer's work as one of the outstanding statements of the practice of Reformed ministers. Baxter is also an example of the Puritan concern for the care of souls. In *The Reformed Pastor,* Baxter emphasizes in particular pastoral visitation and the importance of the pastor's knowing the members of the congregation by name. Yet he defined pastoral care in language that is very theological.

> The ultimate end of our pastoral oversight, is that which is the ultimate end of our whole lives; even the pleasing and glorifying of God, and the glorification of His Church. And the nearer ends of our office, are the sanctification and holy obedience of the people of our charge, their unity, order, beauty, strength, preservation and increase; and the right worshipping of God, especially in the solemn assemblies.
>
> The subject matter of the ministerial work is, in general, spiritual things, or matters that concern the pleasing of God, and the salvation of our people. It is not about temporal and transitory things. Our business is not to dispose of commonwealths, nor to touch men's purses or persons by our penalties; but it consisteth only in these two things:
>
> 1. In revealing to men that happiness, or chief good, which must be their ultimate end.
>
> 2. In acquainting them with the right means for the attainment of this end, and helping them to use them, and hindering them from the contrary.[4]

John Calvin, Martin Bucer, and Richard Baxter can serve as classical examples of pastoral practice in the Reformed churches. The church life to which they ministered was radically different from that in our day. Yet the temptation to describe church life prior to the last seventy-five years as simple is misleading. Calvin, Bucer, and Baxter all lived in tumultuous times. Moreover, they lived in a situation where people, such as they, faced the possibility of death or exile for their faith. In addition people faced the crises of life without any of the technical skills, medicines, and financial affluence that modify these crises for us.

The church life to which they spoke and to which those after them spoke was in other ways much simpler than ours. Church communities, after the turmoil of the Reformation and the mid-seventeenth century, were generally stable, not mobile. Generations of people lived in one particular place. Information was significantly controlled by the community. No television, no radio, or even newspapers brought alien ideas into the congregation. Movement was limited to walking or riding horseback or buggy or later by train. The official commitments of society were Christian. As far as organized church activities go, church life was very simple.

The church situation, especially that to which the American seminaries ministered, radically changed in the nineteenth century as the structures of society changed. Many activities now became organized, such as foreign missions, home missions, youth work, church schools, and publication of Bibles and church literature. Yet throughout the nineteenth century and the first decade of the twentieth century these activities were carried out for the most part by organizations that were set up independently of the church. The Presbyterian Church U.S. (southern) in the beginning debated whether or not it needed church boards or committees for church work beyond the congregational or presbytery level. Yet beginning in the first half of the nineteenth century, denominations began to create their own particular boards or committees. These new boards and agencies significantly impacted the life of local congregations. The tremendous bureaucratization of Presbyterian churches is, however, largely the work of the last seventy-five years, especially the years since World War II.

Church practice in the nineteenth century did not include much more than the traditional concern of preaching, pastoral care, visitation, care for the sick, ministry to the dying, special ministries amid the crises of human life, and catechizing. Increasingly from the middle of the nineteenth century ministers had the responsibility for church schools to teach the faith and for youth work. Raising money for church budgets now became a new responsibility. Churches had been financed by landowners, by the wealthy. Money had been raised in informal ways to support preaching and the administration of the sacraments, the care of the poor, and the upkeep of buildings. Special offerings began to be given to causes such as world missions, home missions, or the relief of human suffering.

The offering for the support of the church programs was integrated into church worship services in the middle of the nineteenth century over considerable protests. The every member canvass became the program of the Presbyterian Church U.S. in 1910. This new way of financing the church through the contributions of ordinary church members was one of the most significant developments in American church life, and it placed new responsibilities on the minister. Many activities in the church up until World War II were frequently carried out by informal groups who acted on their own and then presented to the church a Montreat (Mountain Retreat Association) in North Carolina (1897) or forty acres of land for Union Theological Seminary. Today, little or no church work is done through informal activities. It is all done through committees that have been officially established and through official program. This change has led to an impoverishment of creativity in the life of the church.

The tremendous increase in the activities of local congregations led to an expansion of the seminary's responsibility to teach future ministers how to give leadership in the work of the church. Church work is no longer ministering simply to the sick and dying but carrying on a whole plethora of activities. One of the chief of these activities is bringing members into the church. This had been done traditionally in America through revivals. By the time of World War II, revivals and protracted meetings no longer functioned as the church's outreach in evangelism. Now evangelism required a much more personal and individual outreach of the church and therefore a very different type of activity. At the end of World War II, visitation evangelism became a standard practice in churches and led to tremendous increase in church growth. Increasingly, church membership increased only with the outreach of the church to individuals and to families.

The seminaries responded as early as the 1920s to the new situation with courses in pastoral care that covered the gamut of church activities. Church practice in the seminary I attended (Columbia Theological Seminary, 1940–1943) and the seminary in which I taught (Union Theological Seminary in Virginia, 1959–1990) was taught by persons who had done in the life of the church with considerable distinction what the seminary called them to teach. The basic course that I took in "pastoral theology" was taught by a distinguished pastor, J. Alvin Orr, who had been pastor of the First United Presbyterian Church in Allegheny, Pennsylvania. He simply told us how he, as a pastor, did the work of church administration, leading the session, ministry to the sick and dying, visitation to bring persons into the membership of the church, and leading the work of the church school. He also told us how ministers should dress and deport themselves when they went to a new pastorate; and he gave much mundane advice as paying your bills at the end of the month and keeping your shoes shined. This course was an invaluable help to me as a pastor. In the 1970s when I grew somewhat concerned about how pastoral theology was being taught, I had my class notes mimeographed and made them available to students. After fifty years the advice of a wise pastor still holds good.

The important point is that the seminary took responsibility for how-to-do-it courses. It is easy now to disparage these courses and to note that they sometimes lack theological depth, but in retrospect their importance becomes clear. Seminary graduates knew how to do what they were paid to do, and they did it with considerable effectiveness. One of the outstanding teachers of practical theology in that era was Paul Vieth at Yale. I remember a distinguished friend of mine on the Yale faculty saying that he once somewhat disparaged Vieth's emphasis on the practical dimensions of Christian education; but after Vieth was succeeded by professors who were more concerned with theology than they were with practice, he saw the wisdom of teaching students how to do the work of the church.

The how-to-do-it courses have lost their place in the seminary curriculum. More and more attention is given to theology, to learning theory, to social studies, and to therapy. The professors who teach these courses are well trained. Their courses are useful in their specialized fields, for example, ministry to alcoholics or learning theory. Yet they do not equip students for the basic tasks of leadership in the church school or in stewardship, for example. Moreover, fewer professors in church practice have a distinguished record in doing what they teach. They may have served as pastors in very limited circumstances or as an associate pastor, but few have had the responsibility for leading in the growth and nurture of a congregation. This is also true in homiletics. Fifty years ago homiletics, the art of preaching, was taught by preachers who had demonstrated in churches that they could preach in such a way as to maintain and build up congregational life. The real test of preaching is not a declamation given without responsibility for the community, but the power of sustained preaching over a period of time to build up and maintain a congregation. Today homiletics is taught largely by people with minimal pastoral experience but with Ph.D.'s in preaching.

Many courses in practical theology today are very useful, but unless they teach seminary students how to give leadership in the organization and development of a church school, how to conduct an every member canvass and increase the stewardship of the congregation, how to preach in such a way as to build up a congregation, how to have an active youth program, how to visit and speak to people to bring them into the organized life of the church, into the context of the means of grace, they fail. No amount of learning theory, no theological wisdom about church practice can ever substitute for simply knowing how to do it. Moreover seminary courses in theology and in Bible and in church history ought to be taught not to educate theologians or biblical scholars or historians but persons competent in those areas whose primary responsibilities is leading a congregation as preacher, pastor, and teacher. Ministers need to know, and they ought to get this from their basic courses, how theology and scripture inform church practice. The proper coordination of courses in theology, Bible, and history with those in practice would reduce the necessity for many courses in the practical field and therefore leave more time for study in the basic disciplines.[5]

Courses in practice have not only shifted from how-to-do-it courses to theory, but they have also moved from pastoral care in the ancient tradition of the church to therapy and counseling.

Counseling and therapy are crucially important, but they cannot be exercised in the church at the expense of pastoral care of the kind that Richard Baxter wrote, namely, visiting people and knowing them by name. Counseling and therapy help individuals, but I do not know of situations in which they have built congregations and churches. In the older tradition the emphasis was on the pastor knowing where these specialized services could be found.

The new emphasis on therapy and counseling at the expense of traditional pastoral care raises a question about competence. Is it not wiser for the church to limit its concern with counseling and therapy to the general competence and commonsense wisdom of mature persons without the intention that the student shall become a counselor or therapist? Would it not be better for the church to advise those who want to make their ministry that of counseling and therapy to go the official channels by earning a Ph.D. in clinical psychology or by becoming a psychiatrist? Therapy is not a field in which we need amateurs; even those with the finest training are not infrequently ineffective.

The development of psychology as a scientific discipline became influential in the latter part of the nineteenth century, especially with the work of Wilhelm Wundt (1832–1920) at Leipzig and William James (1842–1910) at Harvard. Sigmund Freud (1856–1939) caught the attention not only of specialists but of the general public. In Europe the works of Carl G. Jung (1875–1961) and Alfred Adler (1870–1937) as well as those of Fritz Kunkel (1889–1956) and of physicians such as Paul Tournier (1898–) and in England the works of a pastor, Leslie Weatherhead (1893–1976), were widely read and related psychology to problems faced by the pastor. In America numerous works on psychology of religion appeared, for example, J. H. Leuba, *Psychological Study of Religion* (1912); Edward Scribner Ames, *The Psychology of Religious Experience* (1910); James Pratt, *Religious Consciousness* (1920). The most influential book in shaping pastoral psychology in America was clinical in character and based on the author's own experience, *The Exploration of the Inner World* by Anton T. Boisen (1937). Seward Hiltner (1909–1981), at the University of Chicago and later at Princeton Seminary, built on the work of Boisen and on the empirical theological tradition at Chicago. Hiltner found in psychology and clinical studies not only help for the pastor but a new source of theological reflection and knowledge.[6]

These studies in psychology had tremendous impact on the teaching of pastoral theology in Presbyterian seminaries. An analysis of the most widely used texts written by four Americans and three Europeans (major contemporary writers on pastoral counseling) contain no references to classical Christian texts on pastoral care, but they contain 330 references to modern therapies.[7] The new pastoral psychology in utilizing the insights and wisdom of the scientific disciplines greatly modified both the traditional role of the pastor and the understanding of church discipline.

The wisest and best preachers and pastors of the church in every age have utilized the best wisdom they could find in the world as well as in scripture in the care of people. The ancient tradition of spoiling the Egyptians (Exodus 3:21–22) has relevance in the field of psychology. Knowledge of psychology not only gave to the pastors a certification that was accepted in the secular culture; it also gave to them a deeper understanding of human behavior and enhanced skills in ministering to people. Moreover, church members expressed their problems in the language of popular psychology.

Yet for all of its contributions to pastoral care the new knowledge of psychology can easily corrupt the Christian understanding of who a human being is and of what the goal of human life is. Over against the new psychology, Eduard Thurneysen (*A Theology of Pastoral Care*, 1962) insisted that human beings are defined not by psychology but by the Word of God.[8] A human being is uniquely the person who hears God's Word and responds to it. This definition does not nullify the data of social sciences which on their own level are useful. It does mean that the social sciences do not define the work of the pastor however much they may enhance his or her skills. Karl Barth, a friend of Thurneysen, made the same point in his *Church Dogmatics:* "The cure of souls, *cura animarum,* thus means in general concern for the individual in the light of God's purpose for him, of the divine promise and claim addressed to him, of the witness especially demanded of him."[9] In the using of the wisdom of modern psychology, pastoral theology must not forget its own Christian presuppositions.

The presuppositions of secular scientific disciplines radically differ from those of Christian faith. For the Christian the human being is defined by God's purposes not by human intentions or desires. The pastor can utilize the wisdom of psychology and encourage a person to receive the best that modern psychology and psychiatry can offer, but pastors must remember that their own function is something more important than the wisdom of psychology. It is incorporating this wisdom into a Christian perspective and commitment. The work of the pastor is, therefore, both more modest and from the theological point of view more important than that of the psychotherapist. The Christian pastor has a unique function which no knowledge or skill in psychology can replace. In the excitement that the new advances of theology brought, many pastors and teachers of pastoral care were tempted to forget that psychology is useful in the church only in the context of the Christian conviction that human beings truly live and realize their own identity in hearing the Word of God. This also is a critical danger in theological education, as Thomas Oden's analysis of popular texts *Care of Souls in the Classic Tradition* (1983) demonstrates.

The seminary is not alone in the problem of putting together theory and practice. The problem is also present in such diverse activities as social work and welfare.[10] In the seminary, however, some issues are clear. More of the "theory" needs to be found in the biblical and theological courses and more of the ancient practice should be taught in church history courses. Two conclusions are very clear. Theory is not of much use without how-to-to-it courses taught by persons who have done it effectively. Therapy, based simply on empirical sciences, not only corrupts Christian faith but is a disaster for traditional pastoral care.

The critical question for seminary education is a willingness to accept the modest task of teaching practice without which no amount of learning in therapy, or learning theory, or in theology shall amount to much.

The seminaries are confronted by an additional challenge in teaching practice, namely, preparing students for the reality of the local congregations. It is easy on seminary campuses to think that the typical congregation has over five hundred members with secretaries, associates, and a director of Christian education. The fact is that 7,319 congregations, 64 percent of all Presbyterian congregations, have 199 or fewer members. The preparation for ministry in small congregations is in part theological and pastoral, an understanding of the meaning of a call and a willingness to accept a call that requires sacrifice. In addition, the seminary must prepare students for leadership in a church in which there is no professional assistance. This education can only come from faculty who are closely related to the church constituency.

Seminary graduates will be ineffective pastors until they have learned "how to do" the work of evangelism, administration, education from the teaching of a professor who has actually done it *effectively*. No knowledge of theory will ever do the work of the church. Moreover, no skill in "how to do it" is ever a substitute for theology and theory.

5

On Choosing a
Seminary Professor

No decision is more crucial for the church than the choice of a seminary professor. Each seminary professor either increases or decreases the number of people who worship God each Sunday. Each seminary professor influences what worshipers hear or do not hear in the teaching and proclamation of God's word. Yet worshipers in local congregations have less and influence on the choice of those who will educate their pastors. Indeed, in many instances they have no influence at all.

The frightening fact is that a number of seminaries, and particularly their faculties, are increasingly remote from the constituency of the seminary as well as the theological and church tradition of the seminary.

Seminary appointments are now in many instances in the hands of faculty members who may have received none of their education in the institutions of the sponsoring denomination, who are strangers to the constituency of the seminary and who have had no experience, or in any case no experience distinguished by achievement, as pastors.

One origin of the present crisis in the seminary was the commendable desire for some diversity, that is, for persons who did not belong to the constituency and who did not graduate from the institution. Many Presbyterian seminaries in the 1950s and 1960s needed such diversity. The problem arose when those who were called for the sake of diversity began to make the seminary into their own image and to repudiate the traditions that had built and established the seminary.

Insofar as I have observed committees that have had the responsibility for choosing faculties, it is generally true that (1) professors from outside the constituency of the seminary seldom support a choice from the constituency; (2) professors who are not alumni-alumnae seldom support appointment of professors who are alumni-alumnae; (3) professors with little or no pastoral experience seldom support the choice of a professor who has had any effective pastorate; (4) professors of modest gifts seldom support the choice or persons of outstanding gifts; (5) professors who are loosely related to classical Christian faith and to the theological tradition of the seminary do not support the choice of professors who confess the evangelical faith of the ancient creeds and the Protestant confessions and who belong to the seminary's theological traditions.

Seminaries increasingly operate according to the standards of secular education, sometimes through the influence of board members who come from secular education. Secular standards of academic freedom and tenure are applied to seminaries, which means that on some campuses a professor may question such Christian doctrines as God's raising Jesus from the dead, but is prohibited from questioning any dogma of the feminist caucus or the African American caucus or the rubrics of political correctness.

Increasingly no one is now specifically responsible for faculty appointments. Forty years ago presidents of seminaries, at least in the Presbyterian Church U.S., were held accountable. With the changes in recent decades to give power to faculty committees in appointing faculty, a sense of accountability, especially to the church, is lost. Congregations frequently do not know the faculty committees who are appointing teachers for their future preachers, and the faculty committees in many instances know little about the congregations that will call their graduates. Boards no longer express the concern about faculty appointments that they did several decades ago. When a prominent minister, Douglas Vaughan, pastor of the First Presbyterian Church, Wilmington, North Carolina, on the Union Theological Seminary in Virginia board protested appointments during a presidential interim, he was *informed* by the chairman of the board, Samuel Spencer, a former college president, that boards had little to do with faculty appointments. The consequence of these changes is that many seminary faculty appointments have been greatly influenced by committees, made up not infrequently of persons who have little knowledge of the pastorate and who are accountable to no one.

The most radical change in the choosing of seminary faculty is the lost sense of call. A generation ago no one applied for a teaching position or for that matter, a pastorate. An application would have nullified any possibility of a call. In my own experience I did not know Union Theological Seminary was looking for a professor until the president telephoned me and insisted on coming to Auburn, Alabama, to talk with me about a very important matter. The preliminary decisions were made without my knowledge or consultation with me. Today, seminary professors are selected out of applicants, none of whom may be especially qualified. A generation ago seminaries sometimes chose a person of outstanding gifts as demonstrated in a pastorate, and then enabled this person to do the necessary graduate study. The new method of choosing professors out of applicants and under the pressures of political correctness has not helped seminary faculties in educating effective pastors.

Changes in the way of choosing faculties began with a desire for diversity. The result has also been a *loss* of diversity. The new faculty are increasingly ingrown, graduating for the most part from ten or fewer graduate schools.[1] They almost all affirm the dogmas of political correctness. They go to the same professional meetings. In only rare instances does the diversity include evangelicals or persons whose orientation is strongly rooted in the local congregation. In fact in some seminaries the diversity does not include an appreciation of the seminary's own tradition or the theology that informed the growth of the Presbyterian Church in this country until its present decline began.

The result of the radical changes on seminary campuses during the past three decades is the loss of the ability of seminaries to graduate ministers who can evangelize or bring members into the church, who can increase church attendance, who can increase the giving of church members, and who are able to call new congregations into being. It is difficult to understand how any seminary without a single pastor with a record of distinguished achievement in building and nurturing a congregation on its faculty can educate people to be pastors.

When I became a seminary professor in 1959, the faculty with which I taught included persons who had been distinguished pastors (for example, W. T. Thompson, John Newton Thomas, James Appleby among others), and who also were the ablest graduates of the institution, that is, graduates who had finished at the top of their classes. This was also true of the faculty of the seminary I entered in 1940. These conditions are no longer true.

It is worth noting that when universities want coaches for winning football teams, they do not choose their coaches from among Ph.D.'s from the Department of Physical Education in the School of Education, but from those who have demonstrated high levels of competence in playing the game and/or in coaching.

The crisis in the seminaries is not simply a Presbyterian concern. In the United Methodist Church, Geoffrey Wainwright of Duke University and Thomas Oden of Drew University have spoken out very vigorously on the plight of seminary education. Robert Jenson and Carl Braaten, who are Lutherans, have likewise spoken clearly, as has Christopher Seitz, an Episcopalian, in a perceptive article in *First Things* (June–July 1994). These persons represent the highest level in theological education and professional competence, and their judgments have to be taken seriously. Secular critiques have also appeared; for example, the article by Paul Wilkes in *Atlantic Monthly* (December 1990).

Seminaries are no longer under the surveillance of church governing bodies as they were thirty or forty years ago. Members of congregations know far more about the policies and actions of state university boards that are covered by the secular press than they do about the policy and action of the boards of their own seminaries. The only information most church members have concerning seminaries are the public relations releases of the seminary development offices.

The church needs, in our time, ministers and professors who give more to the church than they take out in seminaries and in local pastorates. It has been too easy to live on what others have built. Yet, it is a law of life that once one's inheritance is consumed, one can no longer live on it. So the possibility of living in the church, either on seminary faculties or in local pastorates, on what others have done is beginning now to come to an end.

Ideological concerns and the agendas of special interest groups must also be subordinated to the primary task of the seminary. In choosing seminary professors, the first requirement must be a commitment to Jesus Christ as Lord and Savior and to the faith of the confessions of the church. The second requirement is a record of real, effective participation in the life of the church and in the fellowship of particular congregations. The third is a commitment to educate effective pastors. The fourth is competence to teach the designated subject. After these qualifications have been met, concerns of gender, race, and culture may be addressed. Again, the seminary does not exist to advance one's cause, but to educate effective pastors, first of all for a particular denomination and then for the whole Christian community.

The evaluation of faculties has been increasingly the practice in seminaries as well as colleges, but it is questionable if new evaluation procedures have improved teaching. Professors must be evaluated, but evaluations from marginal students are not likely to be helpful. Very accurate methods of evaluation are available. The evaluator needs only to check the registrar's record to note which courses the ablest and most committed students take when they are free to choose. The most accurate test is the documentable results of a seminary professor's teaching in the work of students in the pastorate who took his or her courses and whom he or she influenced.

Scholarship in recent years has assumed a larger role in the evaluation of faculties and of seminaries. The seminaries do need to emphasize scholarship, but scholarship needs to be defined. In current usage it generally refers to research and to publication. But research may be incompetent and publications of little use. If scholarship is a test of a professor's worth, the word needs definition.

Ernest L. Boyer of the Carnegie Foundation for the Advancement of Teaching suggests we need to remind ourselves "how recently the word research entered the vocabulary of Higher Education. It was first used in England in the 1870s by reformers who wished to make Cambridge and Oxford not only a place of teaching, but a place of learning."[2] It was introduced in American education by Daniel Coit Gilman of Johns Hopkins University.

A broader definition of scholarship is needed, Boyer insists. He distinguishes (1) a scholarship of discovery that closely resembles research, (2) a scholarship of integration that puts isolated facts in perspective, (3) a scholarship of application, a type of scholarship that was practiced in land-grant colleges with remarkable competence, and (4) a scholarship of teaching that makes it possible for knowledge to be understood by others. As Aristotle said, "Teaching is the highest form of understanding."[3]

All faculty, Boyer insists, should establish their credentials as researchers. They must demonstrate "the capacity to do original research, study a serious intellectual problem, and present to colleagues the results." Certainly this competence is *essential* for a seminary professor, especially in the basic disciplines. Seminaries cannot compromise these criteria in the selection of faculty.[4]

Boyer goes on to argue that professors should stay in touch with developments in their fields and remain professionally alive. Again seminaries cannot compromise on this point.

Seminaries, however, need other competencies. "Popular writing" that makes available to nonspecialists or to ordinary Christian believers the best thought is very much needed and very difficult. Heiko Obermann, one of the most competent theological scholars of this century, has praised writing that is accessible to any intelligent reader and that a technical scholar can recognize as a precise statement of the church's theology without all the clutter of the study. Not many seminary professors can or have been urged to write "popular theology" that is *profound* and *precise* and at the same time *accessible* to any intelligent reader.

Seminaries must insist that all faculty have the "capacity to do original research, study a serious intellectual problem, and to present to colleagues the results." Yet the seminary must reward other expressions of theological excellence, such as skills in integration and perspective, application and teaching. In no case should a seminary encourage the mediocritizing of any form of scholarship. It must be always remembered that real scholars are few and creative theologians are fewer.

Seminaries must search for a faculty of human maturity and experience. They must also search for professors who have a broad range of intellectual competence and the capacity to make the church's best theology accessible to church members. This capacity to engage in serious theological study and to make the church's best theology accessible to ordinary believers is very rare, but crucial for the church.

The seminary's primary earthly allegiance to which all other organizational allegiances are subordinated is the church. Accrediting associations and the various academic organizations have served useful purposes, but their concerns are increasingly secular, subject to current ideologies and trends. In the life of the seminary, an institution of the church to educate pastors for the church, secular organizations including an association of theological schools must always be secondary.

No one is good enough or wise enough to be a seminary professor. I was often told by my mother and also once by President Jimmy Carter, when I had the invocation for a Jefferson-Jackson Day dinner at which he was the speaker, that teaching theology must be a frightening responsibility. And so it is. All who teach in a seminary must live by justification by faith. But having said that, we must do the best we can.[5]

6

The Moral Use
of Endowments

The church today increasingly lives on the gifts of the dead that were given in trust and received in trust. The use of money that one did not earn or did not give is always a decisive test of personal integrity and responsibility. The pressures toward responsibility are considerable when the user earns or gives the money. The encouragement to responsibility when the money was given by someone else and especially when given by a person who is dead becomes less pressing.

The gifts of the dead to the Presbyterian Church are very considerable. In 1995 Presbyterian congregations reported investment income of $142,751,707 and bequests of $74,212,502. The Presbyterian Foundation dispensed $27,162,720 from income from endowments to the Presbyterian General Assembly, and it also dispensed $5,510,570 to local churches, presbyteries, synods, and institutions.[1] The Presbyterian seminaries are likewise, relative to other seminaries, exceptionally well endowed. Six of the fifteen best-endowed theological seminaries in America are Presbyterian.

Much of the money the church raises today also comes from the labors of people who are now dead. In seminary campaigns bequests are a significant portion of the money raised. Furthermore, living people contribute most frequently on a basis of what they have experienced in the past, on the basis of what the seminary and church programs were several decades ago.

The further the use of money is removed from the surveillance of those who earned it and gave it, the fewer are the external restraints on the irresponsible use of that money. One of, if not the greatest, moral perils in the leadership of the church is the temptation to irresponsibility in the use of money that other people earned and gave. The use of money that one did not earn or give is a decisive test of moral character.

Seminaries easily forget that most of the money they spend was originally given by church people, many of whom were in relatively humble circumstances and most of whom were probably less well paid than seminary professors. The moral issues come to focus in the use of endowments, that is, in the use of gifts that were given in trust and received in trust. Someone may protest that much of seminary endowments today is due to investments and the increase in the Dow Jones average. This is true, but there would have been no money to have increased in value, if it had not been given by someone who earned it. The *social righteousness* and the *prophetic* witness of a seminary are nowhere better revealed than in its use of endowments, keeping with integrity its commitments to those who gave the money.

The role of gifts and endowments in American education go back to the very beginning of higher education in America. Development officers today have not advanced much beyond those energetic money raisers, who were no doubt less well paid, who went to England and across the country looking for money for Harvard, Yale, Princeton, and other institutions. These early money raisers appealed to very worthy motives. John Eliot, for example, a missionary to the Indians and an early member of the Massachusetts Bay Company, reminded a well-to-do Englishman that "if we nourish not learning both church and commonwealth will sink." But then Eliot was capable of going beyond this appeal to other motivations. He finally reminded Simonds D'Ewes that a gift would perpetuate the donor's name, an appeal that was obviously directed to vanity and pride. The solicitors had available not only teaching chairs but also institutions. No two people in the history of philanthropy have ever gotten so much name recognition for so little as John Harvard and Elihu Yale.[2]

The question of integrity in the use of funds was also present from the very beginning. Thomas Hollis, a devout Baptist, was a very generous benefactor of Harvard, establishing the Hollis Chair of Divinity. Hollis was greatly concerned not to impose a Baptist on Harvard as a professor of divinity. Yet he did not want to prevent a Baptist from ever holding the chair. He insisted that none be refused on account of his beliefs and the practice of adult baptism, if he be sober and religiously inclined. Hollis was concerned for the Christian religion rather than for the Christian sect. The diarist Samuel Sewall opposed Hollis's insistence and explained that "the Qualifications of the divinity professor, is to me, a bribe to give my sentence in disparagement of infant baptisme: and I will endeavor to shake my hands from holding it." Sewall would have turned down the philanthropist's gift, but the overseers having the money in hand chose to circumvent the donor's intentions.[3] Thomas Hollis was never fully apprised of the extent to which the spirit of his gift was distorted by its recipients, but he suspected something of the sort.[4]

The problem of integrity in the use of money is further accentuated when one recalls that gifts to institutions such as Princeton, Yale, and Harvard grew out of Christian devotion and were given for the furtherance of the Christian religion. Now those institutions are thoroughly secular with little memory of their past. Without their past, however, they would not be the great universities that they are today. This raises a serious moral question as to the integrity of those who provide leadership even in the most prestigious educational institutions in the use of money.

Protestants from the beginning have been nervous about endowments. The Reformed church had seen the peril of the concentration of endowments in cathedrals and institutions to the neglect of the people in the congregation. Endowments undermined responsibility and service. They encouraged self-serving purposes and indolence.

Robert Kingdon has described the Reformation in Geneva as a social revolution, or, as could be said today, a radical downsizing of the bureaucratic structure of the church. The clergy had become a highly privileged social elite. About one thousand persons were attached to the church in Geneva including lay workers. The Reformation reduced the staff of the Genevan church that now ranged from nine to twenty-two ministers. This was a radical downsizing and also a radical reduction in the number who lived off church revenues.[5]

The Reformation recognized the perils of privileged groups in the church and of endowed moneys to create what, in contemporary language, could be called a welfare class of church bureaucrats. The emphasis of the Reformation was on vocation to service in the church and a rendering of service *without* fees to real people on the congregational level. All of this has significance for institutions that run on endowed moneys from the congregation. The bureaucratization of the institution must be kept at a minimum and the institution's expenditures must be directed to the service of the people on the congregational level. When congregations and institutions are financed by the people, accountability is immediate. When services are not rendered, the money is cut off. Endowments allow church leadership to ignore, if they choose, the people. They also allow the people to evade their responsibility to support the work of the church.

The Reformation in Scotland was a protest against the use of church revenues, not for the maintenance of the congregation but for the maintenance of the church's institutions, organizations, and elite clergy. Revenues not derived from the people are always a temptation to selfish abuse by organizationally elite clergy.[6]

Endowments, however, are a practical necessity for educational institutions such as the seminaries. Institutions require a steady source of income that cannot always be guaranteed by congregational contributions. The question then arises, How can endowments be properly used in a Protestant context and with moral integrity? At least four points seem clear:

1. The first responsibility in the stewardship of endowments is to use the endowments for the purposes for which they were given. Difficulties in literally fulfilling this commitment may arise, but they ought not to be exaggerated. The use of endowments may have to be modified by changes in our society. Yet any modifications ought to point in the same direction and fulfill the same purpose.

The real difficulty in the use of endowments arises when the basic purpose of the endowment is violated. This is especially true when it involves the foundations of the Christian faith. Money that has been given in the conviction that Jesus Christ is the embodiment of the wisdom and the power of God and that in Jesus Christ, God acted decisively for the salvation of all people must always be honored without any deceit.

2. Endowments raise not only questions as to the responsibility in their use but also questions as to the attitude of those who are the beneficiaries of endowments toward the endowments and toward the benefactors. The only proper response to endowments is humility, gratitude, and a certain awe that persons of sometimes limited means

are willing to give so much of their substance for the work to which we in the seminaries put our hands. These attitudes become all the more crucial when account is taken of the sacrifices of those who built the seminaries and those who gave the endowments. Many of them were relatively humble people with relatively low salaries, and they gave their money out of deep conviction and commitment to Jesus Christ.

Endowed chairs have been a source of income for seminaries. Supporters of seminaries like to give funds to honor professors whose contribution to the church they admire. Families like to honor their own distinguished teachers, ministers, or elders. In accepting money for endowed chairs, seminaries obligate themselves to honor the work of persons such as Charles Hodge, Benjamin Warfield, Cyrus McCormick, or Ernest Trice Thompson. Should a seminary accept money for an endowed chair if the seminary does not wish to celebrate the honoree's work in the living tradition and community of the seminary's life? The occasional rejection of a call to a chair by professors who knew that their theology contradicted the theology of the person the chair honored is a tribute to the professor's integrity but an indictment of the institution.

3. Any proper response to endowments must include openness. The records of endowments should be publicly available and open to the constituency of the church. Moreover the seminaries ought to give accountability reports insofar as this is possible, not only to the givers but also to the churches. In any case openness as to the purpose and stipulations of endowments and in the use of the endowments in the fulfillment of those purposes should be a very high priority.

4. Morality in the use of endowments also impacts the solicitation of funds. Seminaries more than secular institutions have an obligation to be scrupulously honest in the way in which they present the seminary and in what they promise the donor. Moreover fund-raisers, administrators, and trustees have an obligation to be sure that they can deliver what they promise.

The problems and the complexities in the moral use of endowments become clearer with actual illustrations of the issues and the problems.

The problem in the use of endowments has been well illustrated in the record of the McNair Lectures at the University of North Carolina at Chapel Hill. A young Presbyterian minister John Calvin Mc-

Nair set up the lectureship in 1857 stipulating that the trustees "shall employ some able scientific Gentlemen to deliver before all the students entered in attendance at the University a course of lectures the object of which Lectures shall be to show the mutual bearing of science and theology upon each other & to prove the existence and attributes (as far as may be) of God from nature." It also stipulated that the lectures must be prepared by a member of one of the Evangelical denominations of Christians.

The university interpreted this will in a very broad sense, inviting lecturers such as John Dewey, who spoke on the "Philosophy of Politics." "In 1926 the Synod of North Carolina of the Presbyterian Church U.S. adopted a memorial [a statement] concerning the university's failure to carry out the purpose of the lectureship and presented it to a representative group of faculty in person to a committee appointed for that purpose."[7] When this was ineffective the matter was brought to the attention of the trustees by a communication of the chairman of the synod's committee and the result was that the trustees and faculty pledged themselves to make the "lectures what McNair intended them to be." At this point Harris Kirk, pastor of the Franklin Street Presbyterian Church, Baltimore, was invited by Dr. Frank Graham to give the lectures.[8]

Unfortunately the protest of the synod to the University of North Carolina was not long-lasting, and in more recent years faculty committees with little acknowledgment as to the original intent of the lectures have invited persons such as Stephen Jay Gould of Harvard, a naturalist, to give the lectures. The University of North Carolina has again been called to accountability by the heirs of John C. McNair. Once again a pledge has been made that the lectures will fulfill their purpose. A notable recent lecture was given by John Polkinghorne, a devout Christian and a distinguished theoretical physicist. Robert J. Powell, Jr., a McNair descendant, has received cooperation from the university authorities and the full support of the chancellor, Dr. Michael K. Hooker, in his recent efforts to establish the McNair Lectures on a foundation that honors the purpose of the donor.[9]

The record of the McNair Lectures at the University of North Carolina represents the kind of irresponsibility that goes on in academic institutions in the use of money given in trust and received in trust. This irresponsibility does not arise necessarily from evil intentions but more likely from indifference to questions of morality in the use of endowments by persons holding the highest positions in the academic world.

Theological seminaries have the same problem. A few years ago the development department at Union Theological Seminary in Virginia proposed a chair to be named for my retired colleague John Newton Thomas, being aware of the resources available to his family and friends that could help finance it. When I was asked to support this, I gave enthusiastic approval but enthusiastic only on one basis, namely, that the occupant of the chair would have to have some continuity in theology and churchmanship with John Newton Thomas. I insisted that this was necessary for integrity. My suggestion was rejected. The seminary pursued the matter and secured the one million dollars. The announcement of the naming of this professorship was done by the Dean and Professor of Ethics at Union Seminary at the church in which Professor Thomas and I worship. I am sure that those who heard the announcement assumed that this professorship would carry on the tradition of John Newton Thomas. Now that the seminary has this named professorship, it is in the position of having no one in the theology department who is in continuity with either the churchmanship or the theological commitments of John Newton Thomas. It will be interesting to observe how the seminary will work out the basic morality and sense of appropriateness in naming someone to this chair.

The very serious problems that arise with the use of endowments has been illustrated in two recent bequests to Columbia Theological Seminary. John Bulow Campbell, a prominent Atlanta businessman and elder, was a leader in the movement of Columbia Seminary from Columbia, South Carolina, to Decatur, Georgia, in 1928. Apart from his benefaction and leadership this move could not have been accomplished. He was theologically conservative, according to his daughter, Virginia Courts (in a letter of October 21, 1992, addressed to the Board of Columbia Theological Seminary), and was concerned for the future of Presbyterianism in the southeastern region of the United States. John Bulow Campbell in his will written in 1935, before his death in 1940, left to Columbia Seminary the income from what in 1995 had become fifty-five million dollars. The problem is set by the fact that there is very little continuity between the Columbia Seminary that exists today, either in administration or in faculty, with the Columbia Seminary that John Bulow Campbell knew. What is the moral use of endowments given to a seminary that now no longer exists in the form that the donor knew? The answer to this is not simple, but there has to be, if moral integrity is to be maintained, a real substantial continuity between what John Bulow Campbell intended and what is now happening on the Columbia Theological Seminary campus.

The continuity of living traditions and communities is very resilient as well as fragile. They have built-in factors of inertia. Many have survived centuries and millennia. Yet even the resilient traditions that have survived for centuries exhibited a certain fragility in the post–World War II world in which many forces impact individuals as well as communities.

All seminaries were established by living communities and traditions, and they too exhibited amazing resilience to radical change up until World War II. Yet seminaries as they are organized today are far more fragile than communities. The seminary today is more an organization than can radically change its direction in a short time with a few organizational decisions. Seminary faculties fifty years ago were searched out and called by the seminary from its supporting community. In more recent years seminary faculties have been chosen, not out of the supporting constituencies, but out of Ph.D. applicants, some of whom have little connection with the constituency or the traditions of the seminary. Increasingly, seminary faculty are chosen by committees of faculty who themselves did not come out of the traditions of the seminary, have little commitment to those traditions, and have little personal or financial investment in the seminaries or the communities for which they are choosing new faculty. The result is that the seminary becomes an organization rather than a community, an expression of the community of faith for which it is preparing pastors. In a short period of a decade or so the whole direction of a seminary can be radically changed, so that only the buildings, the library, and the endowment maintain its connection with the past out of which it came to be, or with the community for which it is supposed to educate persons who can be pastors who will build and nurture churches. The moral issues raised by the John Bulow Campbell endowment will grow increasingly serious, until seminaries take seriously the task of maintaining continuity with the traditions and communities out of which the seminaries came. This means appointing faculty out of the community, who love the community and seek to nurture it.

The second illustration is also from Columbia Theological Seminary. William Marcellus McPheeters, professor of Old Testament from 1888 to 1932, was not only an influential teacher but also an influential leader in the Presbyterian Church U.S. He was theologically on the very right wing and was one of the most effective leaders in the growth of fideistic fundamentalism in the Presbyterian Church U.S.[10] He was active in promoting the heresy charge (1928–1934) against Hay Watson Smith, pastor of the Second Presbyterian Church, Little Rock, Arkansas.[11]

Professor McPheeters' son, Thomas McPheeters of Charlotte, North Carolina, left a trust established with North Carolina National Bank, on February 20, 1961, to Columbia Theological Seminary that on the death of his wife amounted to approximately five million dollars. In announcing this gift *Vantage* (spring 1990), the Columbia Theological Seminary magazine, declared it was the largest gift in the school's 162-year history. President Douglas Oldenburg declared that no one currently at Columbia could take credit for the gift. The board established the William Marcellus McPheeters Chair of Old Testament Studies. President Oldenburg declared that the gift would be used "to assure the long range health of the seminary."[12] No announcement was ever made about any stipulations of the trust. It is known, however, that J. McDowell Richards, president of the seminary (1932–1971), a man generally regarded as possessing great integrity, was troubled in conscience each year when he signed a statement that the seminary was teaching the doctrines of the Westminster Confession, as he was uncertain that the teachings at Columbia were in complete harmony with the Westminster Confession as the trust required for the funds the seminary was then receiving.[13]

The Westminster Confession of Faith is still one of the doctrinal standards of the church. What does the acceptance of this money by Columbia Theological Seminary mean for its affirmation of the Westminster Confession of Faith? What does it mean in the naming of a person to hold the William Marcellus McPheeters Chair of Old Testament Studies?

These questions are hard and difficult to answer, but they lie at the heart of the moral integrity of a seminary that has received funds that were given in trust and that were received in trust. They can only be answered as seminaries maintain the integrity of the traditions and communities out of which they came. (For an illustration from Princeton Theological Seminary, see note 14 on page 123.)[14]

7

Seminary Constituencies and Boards

D oes the seminary need a constituency? Is the seminary an integral part of a larger community? Is the seminary a freestanding institution appointing its own trustees and charting its own future? Is such a freestanding institution any longer possible?

The Seminary Constituency

The historical answer to these questions is very simple. Seminaries originated out of the life of the church, out of the work of dedicated ministers and lay people, out of a community that shared a common life. On a technical level the relationship between seminaries and congregations, as was the case with colleges, may not always have been clear. Yet the great reality was the church, a community sharing a common faith and a common sense of ownership in the seminary and college. In such a situation clear-cut definitions were not necessary. Bureaucratic and organizational laws and regulations generally came later when the community was fractured. The relationship between the seminary and the community of worshiping, believing congregations was sustained by a common faith and a shared life. The seminary and the congregations participated in a symbiotic, intimate relationship that grew out of a common faith and its confession.

The relationship between the seminary and a church may be strengthened and helped by church appointment of board members, but the appointment of board members by church governing bodies cannot guarantee it. Presbytery and synod appointments can be as irresponsible as those of a freestanding board, especially as presbyteries themselves become organizations rather than communities and are increasingly under the pressure of quota systems and of special interest groups with their own social agendas. Yet the self-perpetuating board more easily becomes the victim of cause-oriented movements and of current fads than a board appointed by church constituencies. Worse still, a self-perpetuating board may simply become a rubber stamp for the administration.

No organizational action or program can maintain the relationship of a seminary to its constituency or to its tradition. Constituency and tradition are more deeply rooted in human life and community and cannot be created by functional, technological, committee, or organizational decisions.

Our secular, pluralistic culture has revealed what has always been the case. Institutions are very fragile, especially in society since World War II. In this society it is very difficult to guarantee that an institution will continue to grow out of its own tradition and that it will continue to be an institution within the larger community of faith. No organizational power can guarantee it. The only guarantee of an institution's integrity and traditions is to be found in the personal faith and commitments of those who are the seminary and the constituency, who love the institution, believe in it, and support it.

In recent years seminaries have lost contact with their constituencies. They have increasingly become independent university-type schools. Some seminaries whose boards were once appointed by church governing bodies now have self-perpetuating boards. This trend was accentuated by the reorganization of the church in the 1970s and 1980s. Union Theological Seminary in Virginia had until 1986 a board nominated by church courts. The change from a church-nominated board to a self-appointing board was not noticed at the time. No one in the seminary constituency raised questions concerning the long-range consequences of this decision. Indeed no one publicly raised any questions about whether or not a self-perpetuating board would be faithful to those who had built the institution and endowed it for a specific purpose. As a faculty member, I must confess to negligence as a presbyter in not being sufficiently aware of what was happening in my own institution.

In 1986 the General Assembly of the Presbyterian Church (U.S.A.) adopted a report on the status of theological seminaries in the new denominational structure. The report presupposed a presentation by Robert Lynn that emphasized the role of scholarship in the seminaries, though it should have been apparent in 1986 that educating effective pastors, not scholarship, was the critical issue in seminaries, as the quantifiable data in church life pointed to the ineffectiveness of seminary graduates as pastors of churches.[1]

The report acknowledged that seminaries were related to the denomination in a variety of ways, and it did not prescribe any one pattern for electing trustees. Diverse ways of electing trustees was affirmed. The election of trustees of seminaries is to be reported to the General Assembly for approval. Charter changes are likewise to be reported to the Assembly. The seminaries, however, are not bound by the General Assembly action. The only sanction is the possible withdrawal of Assembly funding.[2] The long-range consequences of this action and of seminaries related to the churches in the loosest possible way have not been faced.

A number of reasons conspired for the separation of seminaries from their primary constituencies. (1) As has been indicated, seminary faculties were increasingly appointed out of Ph.D. applicants and without any relationship to the constituency of the seminary, and, as has been noted, faculties are becoming very ingrown with graduates of a select few graduate schools. (2) Seminary faculties were increasingly made up of persons who have not had active experience within the pastorate and whose primary vocation is that of scholars. Hence, they were not active in the church as former faculties were. (3) Changes in fieldwork also contributed to the isolation of the seminary. Thirty years ago most students worked during the summers in churches. Union Theological Seminary in Virginia under the leadership of James Appleby had a widespread network of churches that annually had students on their staff during the summer. In more recent decades most students are married and do not find it convenient to engage in this kind of fieldwork. In any case the policies of the seminary have been changed. Too often the relationship of students to churches is preaching on Sunday morning. While this activity is financially rewarding, it is not a good introduction to the work of the church. (4) The public relations of the seminary have become almost indistinguishable from the public relations of a secular college with a sharp focus on money. (5) Faculty members do not now, as much as they once did, serve as pastors to their former students after they leave the seminary. The only relationship many seminary graduates have with their institution is the annual request for money and the reception of public relations mailings. Increasingly they are strangers to the current faculty.

Roland Bainton of Yale once told me he kept in communication with five hundred to six hundred persons. This must be the limit for effective personal relationships. Those who knew Roland Bainton as teacher and then as a friend were enriched not simply by what he taught but by the person he was. In addition this continuing personal relationship formed a constituency for Yale Divinity School.

The breakdown of constituencies is a widely experienced phenomenon within the church. The reorganization of the Presbyterian Church U.S. in the 1970s and the organization of the Presbyterian Church (U.S.A.) in the 1980s have demonstrated that constituencies cannot be constituted by organizational fiat. Committees sitting in an isolated office can prepare charts about how presbytery boundaries ought to be fixed and their decisions may be supported by a great deal of quantifiable demographic data. Yet presbyteries, as communities, cannot be formed by committees, as organizing committees discovered in the 1970s and as subsequent history has confirmed. People have their own connections and they face toward their own communities. For example, a great deal of data could be amassed that churches in the west end of Virginia ought to belong to a presytery in eastern Tennessee, but those who made the boundaries soon discovered this was not possible.

The church on the human level is to a great extent a volunteer organization. Church people on the congregational level do not do anything because they are ordered to by a church governing body or committee. The church has neither a marine corps nor an IRS. It lives by moral suasion.

The reorganizers of the church also discovered that institutional constituencies cannot simply be reconstructed. Excellent committees tried to rearrange college constituencies or unite colleges, but they discovered that this cannot be done by fiat. Communities that support institutions, as well as communities of faith, are created out of life. They are very delicate. They take a long time to develop, and whenever they are destroyed, they are replaced with great difficulty.

Presbyteries in the area the of old Presbyterian Church U.S. still suffer the consequences in financial support and in church activity because the simple nature of communities was not fully understood by people who thought that churches could be organized according to rational patterns and arbitrary committee decisions.

The Synod of North Carolina, for example, in the 1970s was a great community with a long history. When it met, seven hundred or eight hundred people gathered, an event in the public life of North Carolina. Newspapers took the meeting of synod seriously. That is all gone now. The great Synod of North Carolina was supplanted by the much larger Synod of the Mid-Atlantic which gathers a group of seventy-two people, chosen by presbyteries, but frequently not adequately representative of the people in the constituencies. The result is that few people—the newspapers, the public, and unfortunately Presbyterians—pay any attention to the Synod of Mid-Atlantic. It cannot raise money, and it cannot engage in any significant enterprises. Communities of faith and communities that support institutions grow out of life. They take a long time to develop, and they are very fragile.

All of us should have learned that whenever boundaries are changed and committees attempt to arrange communities, the effectiveness of the work of the church is decreased. Sometimes this is necessary, but the cost must be counted. Organizations cannot instruct people what institution they are to support. Support for an institution grows out of community.

Seminary constituencies can be renewed, and they can grow out of shared experiences. No one, however, should underestimate the time and the cost that will have to go into the recovery of constituencies that were so easily discarded since the 1960s.

The significance of constituencies is also seen in the recent history of university-based divinity schools. Without church constituencies they have increasingly become graduate schools or centers for the study of religion. The resources of once major theological schools have tragically declined. The Divinity School at Yale may have to leave its campus, a campus that was only a few decades ago the finest in Christendom. Union Theological Seminary in New York City, in the 1950s surely one of the outstanding institutions in the world, has experienced radical decline, including the sale of some of its property. In the 1950s Union Theological Seminary in New York City

sponsored the finest summer conferences for ministers available anywhere. I still remember a dinner in 1954 when President Henry P.
Van Dusen had at the head table business and political leaders of New
York along with notable church leaders from all over the world who
were on their way to the World Council of Churches meeting in
Evanston, Illinois. I remember thinking that this was a dinner that was
as wonderful as any in church history. The rapid decline of Union
Theological Seminary in New York City as an influence in American church life is both sad and tragic, but illustrative of what is happening in theological education.

The problem of communities is larger than that of the church. A
student of society and a management consultant, Peter Drucker, has
pointed out the fundamental distinction between an organization and
a community.[3] An organization is a tool or a means to an end, a tech-
nology. An organization is functional. A community differs from an
organization. A community is a body of people who share a common
faith, a common manner of life, a common hope, and more than that,
common experiences which they have assimilated from the past and
common experiences in which they themselves have participated.
The church is not an organization but a community, a body of people who share a common life and who support each other. Neither
the church nor the seminary needs any more organization. We have
too much organization, too much bureaucracy now. What the
church and the seminary need is a community, a constituency of tradition, faith, and commitment.

The primary importance of a constituency for a seminary is not organizational. Financial support is secondary. The critical importance
of a constituency of faith and commitment to the seminary lies in the
education of pastors. Only a constituency can provide the context of
worship, of ethos, of commitment, of manner of life, of intentionality and purpose that is essential for the education of pastors. No competency in instruction and no brilliance of academic work can ever
replace the awareness on a seminary campus that it is the part of a believing, worshiping constituency. This symbiotic, intimate relationship cannot be produced organizationally.

The seminary may sponsor many public relations programs, but
the reality of the community that includes the seminary grows out of
life and history.

In retrospect as I look back over my own experience, this point becomes all the more crucial. The seminary I attended did not have at that time a great library and its faculty was very small, but there was on the campus a profound awareness that this was the Presbyterian Church's seminary. Moreover, in the congregations that surrounded this seminary there was likewise an awareness that the seminary was their institution. They nurtured it, they loved it, and they supported it. They expected to call their pastors from it. Here again this kind of relationship grows out of life, as the constituency builds the seminary and as the seminary supports and nurtures the constituency.

When I moved from Columbia Seminary to university-type institutions I rejoiced in the competence in the instruction and the great Christian wisdom of the faculty who taught me, but I felt then as I feel now, that it is very difficult for university-type schools, even with the faculties that existed a generation ago, to maintain the kind of relationship to the church that is crucial. One simple difference is this: the ablest graduates of a theological seminary a generation ago went automatically into the pastorate or mission field. They had to be persuaded to go to graduate school. When I went to a university theological school I suddenly discovered that the ablest students were supposed to take Ph.D.'s and become teachers. This is a subtle but a very real difference. We need institutions of each type in our society. There is, however, no substitute for the *church's* institution training its pastors and for the real presence of the *church* on the seminary campus for the effective education of pastors. This presence cannot be artificially contrived or created by organizational fiat. It grows out of life.

Boards

Boards and constituencies are closely related. Boards should come out of the constituency and should be composed of those persons with the highest documentable qualifications to give leadership to theological education.

Seminary boards differ from college boards. College boards are made up of graduates of the college to a much higher degree than seminary boards. Graduates have a relationship to an institution that is unique. Seminary boards ought to have in their membership the *ablest* and *best* qualified ministers who have graduated, but they must also choose those who are not ministers. This makes the choice of persons to be on a seminary board much more difficult and much more crucial. Lay people do not have the kind of intimate knowledge of the institution, and sometimes the kind of love and commitment that graduates do.

Seminary boards along with most boards in recent years have been greatly weakened by an emphasis on representation, quota systems, and social agendas. Seminary boards ought to have diversity, but diversity is far down the list of requirements. Diversity on the seminary boards, as presently emphasized, does not always include a desire to have on the board strong, able persons who represent the mainstream of the theology that informed the growth of the Presbyterian Church in this country and that still informs most of its growing, vital churches.

The qualifications for being on a seminary board are (1) personal faith and commitment to Jesus Christ as Lord and Savior of life and commitment to the task of the seminary to educate pastors to preach the gospel; (2) a *documentable* record of *effective* work in a local congregation as a member or as a minister; (3) maturity of judgment and life; (4) *documentable* experience in making the kind of serious judgments that seminary boards are required to make and for *anticipating* the consequences of those decisions. Too frequently persons are put on boards who never in their regular lives are called on to make the kind of decisions that boards have to make, and more particularly who are never called on to contemplate seriously the long-range consequences of the decisions they make. As there are no unimportant faculty appointments, so there are very few insignificant board decisions. Most appointments and most decisions have consequences that those who make the decisions and those who make the appointments seldom realize.

After these qualifications have been met questions of diversity can be considered.

Board membership should be regarded as a high responsibility, not as an honor. Board members must be aware that in the long run they shall be held accountable for their stewardship of the contribution and labors of those who built the institution.

Seminary boards, especially those responsible for nominating board members, can with profit ponder this paragraph from *Renewing the Academic Presidency* prepared by a special commission, appointed by the Association of Governing Boards of Universities and Colleges:

Nothing is more critical to the future success of higher education than improving the quality and performance of boards of trustees. For public boards the need is urgent. Governors and legislators should seek only appointees who demonstrate a serious commitment to serving the entire institution and a broad appreciation of the role of higher education. The qualifications for trustees of public institutions should be stated publicly and by law, and governors and legislators should adhere to these qualifications when filling vacancies. Those selected should represent the wide interests of the institution or system, not narrow constituencies or single issues.

The report had preceded this recommendation with the observation that "unfortunately, too many trustees lack a basic knowledge of higher education or a significant commitment to it."

Seminary boards must understand that seminaries are a church institution. Contemporary businessmen almost inevitably bring to board decisions the mentality that governs a secular board of directors. Union Theological Seminary in Virginia recently had two college presidents as chairmen of its boards, but I would argue that neither of them really understood the difference between a seminary as an institution of the church and the college of which they were president or at least their intentions for those colleges. A college is frequently a very secular institution. A seminary is an institution of the church to educate pastors. Its intellectual discipline may be and frequently is very high, but the education of ministers takes place in a community of Christian faith. In any case, from the perspective from which I write and from ratings of the seminary's status, their stewardship of the seminary was a tragedy leading to its decline in status as measured by public ratings and to highly publicized controversies.

Seminary boards ought to have the ablest lay people in the constituency, but they must also include strong and able ministers. Union Theological Seminary, where I taught, has been run by a lay leadership for at least two decades. Active ministers, who have been outstanding ministerial graduates of the seminary, have been persistently kept off of the executive committee. A recent committee to name a president for Union Theological Seminary in Virginia was dominated by lay persons and non–Union Seminary graduates (B.D. or M.Div.). It did not include any Union Seminary graduate with the influence of a national or denominational reputation for building churches or for scholarship. This means either that the seminary is run by the administration for whom the executive committee is something of a rubber stamp, or that the executive committee is running an institution about which it lacks firsthand knowledge. In my experience seminary boards too often depend on what the administration tells them without having the knowledge critically to evaluate what they are told.

The success of a seminary will increasingly depend on its boards. No substitute exists for having able lay people who in daily life are making the kind of decisions they are called on to make at the seminary. Board members must also be real church people. Boards ought to include the seminaries' ablest graduates appointed for their competence in general, for their *documentable* achievement, and for their far greater knowledge of the seminary. The failure of Union Theological Seminary in Virginia to give this kind of serious attention to board appointments has been, in my judgment, one of the reasons for its decline.

Every seminary board ought to be reminded continually that membership on the board is not an honor, not an opportunity for individual board members to do their own thing or to try to capture the resources of the church for their own social agendas, but a great responsibility for stewardship of money that has been entrusted for the primary purpose of educating pastors.

Great constituencies and great board members cannot be created by organizational procedures. They come out of communities with long histories. The great lay members of the Union Theological Seminary Board, whom I have known, all had long histories of service in the church.[4] They came out of families and churches with long histories of support for the seminary and the church. They were also persons of the *highest* achievement in their chosen fields of work. They were not appointed to the seminary board to meet requirements of political correctness, or of current advocacy movements, or because of wealth, though some were obviously wealthy and leaders in the top echelons of business. They were church people, and they were persons of distinguished achievement.

The renewal of the seminary will come out of the recovery of the church as a community of authentic Christian faith and fellowship. This communal context has been easy to lose in a pluralistic, secular society. The recovery will be slow.[5]

8

The Recruitment of Students

Any serious discussion of the calling of persons into the Christian ministry must begin with an analysis of the changes that have occurred in our society and their impact on the calling of persons into the ministry. The secularization of the church has also brought significant changes both in ministerial decorum and in the activity of the church in calling persons to be pastors.

The New Situation

The first notable change in the recruitment of a minister grows out of the secular understanding that the church has jobs to which certain persons are entitled. One of the saddest signs in the decline of the church are the pages of advertisements in the *Presbyterian Outlook* of churches seeking to find ministers. Of equal sadness is the necessity of young ministers applying for jobs, filling out personal information forms, going to face-to-face programs, and aggressively pursuing positions in the pastorate. Young seminary graduates today are caught in a system that by its very nature is destructive of the sense of the call, of personal dignity, and of the church as a community of faith.

Older ministers can remember that open pursuit of a call to a pastorate or to a seminary professorship was a sure way of being eliminated from consideration for the call. The new system of "calls" is further complicated by presbytery procedures and by the oversight of presbytery committees, sometimes made up of persons of minimal documentable competence to advise churches on the calling of ministers. There is no evidence that the elaborate system of "calling" ministers that is now in place is as effective as the old way when churches, having named a highly competent committee, were relatively free to proceed to call a pastor.

The system that is at work in the church is also at work in the "calling" of persons to seminary professorships. A generation ago the seminary took the initiative in finding the person they wanted for a professorship and then calling that person to the task. Today whenever a professorship becomes vacant the seminary is flooded with applications.

This secularization and bureaucratization of the church has led to a lost sense of a call and to the notion that the ministry is like any other secular work, that the calling of a minister, as members of pulpit nominating committees have noted, is not different from hiring a person for GE or GM. Over against these trends, it should be emphasized that the church is not in the business of providing jobs for people and that the seminary is not a trade school.

Other trends in the recruitment of students to the seminary have likewise undercut a passionate sense of the call to preach the gospel. Some have looked on seminaries as therapeutic communities, having experienced the nurture and support of congregations, and they go to the seminary for nurture and support, forgetting that the seminary at its best requires rigorous discipline and quality performance in preparation for the arduous tasks of the pastorate.[1] No one goes to the University of Virginia Law School looking for a support group or nurture. But students do come to seminaries looking for support. Seminaries ought to be wholesome communities in which to live, but they are not first of all nurturing and supporting communities.

Others come to the seminary because of social agendas, and in recent years seminary communities have been more favorable to social advocates and their agendas than other communities.

These changes in the seminary have also paralleled the change in the status of the ministry. In the years since World War II ministers have become a relatively protected people with considerable job security and benefits. None of this could have been anticipated prior to World War II. The Presbyterian Church U.S. adopted a pension program in 1940. Ministers became eligible for Social Security in 1953. Health insurance became common and later mandatory in the 1960s. Today calls to churches specify minimal salaries along with pension, Social Security, health insurance, book allowances, study leaves, and vacation. Persons entering the ministry prior to World War II did not anticipate the minimum salaries, the benefits, and the job security that ministers now have. The changes that have come in the support of the ministry are all well intentioned and in most cases deserved. Yet it is quite clear that the decision to become a minister does not involve the decision to sacrifice and risk that such a vocational decision did up until World War II.

The problem of compensation for ministers is very difficult. The apostle Paul struggled with it. On the one hand, he knew that the minister was worthy of his hire, but on the other hand, he always wanted to pay his own way so that no one could say that he was paid for preaching the gospel. (2 Thessalonians 3:6–10).

Reinhold Niebuhr in 1924 stated the dilemma confronting the minister and the minister's salary with incisive clarity.

> The idea of a professional good man is difficult enough for all of us who are professionally engaged as teachers of the moral ideal. Of course "a man must live"; and it is promised that if we seek first the kingdom and his righteousness "all these things shall be added unto us." But I doubt whether Jesus had a $15,000 salary in mind. If things that are added become too numerous they distract your attention terribly. To try to keep your eye on the main purpose may only result in making you squint-eyed. I hope the new prophet won't begin his pastorate with a sermon on the text, "I count all things but loss."[2]

The benefits and the securities that are now guaranteed to ministers can serve excellent purposes, but they are also temptations to sloth. The intention to provide study leave and book allowances is wholly good, but I do not know of any evidence that the generous book allowances and study leaves that are now guaranteed by churches have resulted in greater biblical and theological competence than was true of ministers before these allowances and study leaves were made available. As for salaries it is obvious that moral responsibility demands that the person who receives a salary should earn it whether it is small or large. The vocation of a minister is not to a comfortable life and job security, but to preach the gospel of what God has done and to nurture a congregation, a calling that has its rewards but that also requires sacrifice.

The problems created by the secularization of the seminary and of the church have been greatly accelerated by trends in our secular culture, endangering the classic Christian doctrine of the call to the ministry. The problem however is not new.

An Old Discussion
Gives Perspective

A discussion of the call to the ministry that took place one hundred fifty years ago between two great Presbyterian ministers, James Henley Thornwell (1812–1862) and Robert J. Breckinridge (1800–1871) sets the contemporary problem in clearer relief.

Thornwell, in an article titled, "The Call of the Ministry" (1847), responded to a pamphlet by Breckinridge on the nature of the ministerial call. Breckinridge and Thornwell alike agreed on the fundamental emphasis on the call of God. "It is a prerogative of God, and of God alone, to select the men who shall be invested with authority in His Church; and the validity of this Divine call is evinced to others and rendered satisfactory to ourselves by the testimony of our own consciences, the approbation of God's people and the concurrence of God's earthly courts. Conscience, the Church, the Presbytery—these do not call into the ministry but only declare God's call; there are the forms in which the Divine designation is indicated—the scriptural evidences that he who possesses them is no intruder into the sacred ministry."[3]

Thornwell was very much opposed to the doctrine of the American Education Society that every young man of talents and attainments should devote himself to the ministry without some special reason to the contrary.

No one, Thornwell insisted, should go into the ministry unless he feels compelled to. "The true doctrine is that no man, whether young or old, rich or poor, learned or unlearned, should presume to dispense the mysteries of Christ without the strongest of all possible reasons for doing so—the imperative, invincible call of God. No one is to show cause why he ought *not* to be a minister: he is to show cause why he *should* be a Minister. His call to a sacred profession is not the absence of a call to any other pursuit; it is direct, immediate, powerful to this very department of labor. He is not here because he *can* be no where else but he is no where else because he *must* be here."[4]

Thornwell and Breckinridge were in the tradition of Calvin in emphasizing that the first qualification of the ministry was "that secret call, of which each minister is conscious before God, and which does not have the church as its witness."[5] Yet neither Calvin nor Thornwell believed that a person's conviction of having been called to be a minister was sufficient. There were other tests. "Learning joined with piety and the other gifts of the good pastor" must be evident.[6] Those whom God destines for the high office of pastor, he supplies with the gifts necessary to fulfill it.

The call must also be confirmed by a responsible church authority that in Presbyterianism is the presbytery. Calvin also insisted on the vote of the people in calling a pastor. The right of the people to elect their pastors was affirmed by Calvin in the very beginning of the Reformation, but it became possible only after many hard battles with landowners, church authorities, and government. It was won only in the late eighteenth and nineteenth centuries. It was clearly written into the old books of church order: the inalienable right of the people to elect those who govern them and who preach to them. Today this right is again being lost to presbytery procedures and to a quota system. Congregations have very little direct input into the calling of the ministers, though no minister can be effective as a pastor without the approbation of the people of God.

The test of the call to the ministry was not simply the vote of the people but the approbation of the people over a period of time that came to expression in the actual voting for a minister or for elders. This test, the approbation of the people of God over a period of time, is the most reliable, but it is very difficult to apply to a candidate for the ministry or at the time of ordination.

No sign is ever an infallible indication of the divine call. Many signs such as learning joined to piety may support the call. Of all the fallible signs of the authenticity of a call none is of greater value than the approbation of the people of God, who through a period of time become increasingly convinced that the minister in preaching, teaching, and pastoral care gives evidence of having been called by God.

This emphasis on the primary importance of the divine call should temper and modify any procedures and methods the seminary or the organized church may use to call persons into the ministry. The recruitment of theological seminary students must be in agreement with the church's doctrine of the ministry and in particular with the church's doctrine of the church.

Thornwell and Breckinridge alike were hesitant to take the initiative in encouraging people to become ministers, especially in encouraging people indiscriminately to become ministers. As Breckinridge put it, "It is easy for us to multiply ministers of the gospel, but it is impossible for us to multiply such as are called by God."[7] Thornwell likewise was hesitant, and he knew that we cannot make ministers out of those who have not been called. "The characteristic qualification for the ministry, the unction from on high, is the immediate gift of the Holy Ghost and cannot be imparted by any agency of man. Human learning is necessary—the more, the better; but human learning cannot, of itself, make a preacher."[8]

Breckinridge and Thornwell were also skeptical of aid programs for theological students. Schemes to stimulate the calling forth of ministers and to increase the numbers are fraught with dangers. "Such schemes," Breckinridge wrote, "to say the very least, seem not so much directed to enquiries for such as God has called, as to experiments which may ascertain if He has not called a multitude besides. And it surely increases the danger greatly that youths in the first stages of religious experience—of tenders years, of circumstances in which a gratuitous education is itself a very powerful temptation, and the station of a Minister of the Gospel a seduction nearly irresistible—are, to a great extent, the object of these experiments. Suppose them to succeed perfectly, and the result is almost inevitably a class-ministry and what is worse still an eleemosynary [welfare] class-ministry."[9]

Breckinridge went on to say that he was in favor of providing aid to those who are called to be pastors, but he was opposed to throwing the door wide open.

Thornwell concludes, "We are satisfied that the whole system of urging, as it is called, the claims of the ministry upon the minds of the young is inconsistent with just and scriptural views of its nature and duties. To preach the gospel is a privilege, a distinction, and it has consequently claims upon no one until he possesses satisfactory evidence that he is entitled to the honor. It is the *call* which makes it his duty, and until the call is made known there can be no pressure of conscience about it."[10]

How do these words of Calvin about the ministry and the discussion of two great Presbyterian ministers of one hundred fifty years ago affect our understanding of the recruitment of pastors today? They are so in conflict with the way we have come to think and to speak about the calling of ministers that they shock us. The shock should remind us that we need to give deeper thought to the nature of the ministry and to the call to it.

The Loss of the
Context of the Means of Grace
in Which the Call to the Ministry Ordinarily Came

These words of wisdom from the past, however we may apply them today, should make clear that the calling of ministers does not come through public relations schemes or organizational activities or marketing but out of the community of faith itself. The calling of the minister comes in the context of the ordinary, intentional means of grace—in the Christian family and in the Christian church. God's grace is sovereign. God calls when and where he chooses. Yet I can testify, on the basis of many years of teaching, that students learn the nature of the church by growing up in it and acquiring from this life in the church a knowledge, an understanding, and a wisdom that simply cannot be taught by seminaries.

John Calvin always insisted that the activities of the church must take place in a context in which there is an awareness of the holy. Certainly this is true in the calling of people into the ministry. Calvin's words concerning the calling of a person to a pastorate are applicable in the more general sense to calling people to the ministry. Calvin says that the adverb "how" in the calling of the minister refers not so much to the ceremony of choosing but "to religious awe, which ought to be observed in the act of choosing. Hence, fasting and prayers, which Luke relates the believers used when they created presbyters. For, since they understood that they were doing the most serious thing of all, they dared attempt nothing but with the highest reverence and care. But they especially applied themselves to prayers, in which they besought from God the Spirit of counsel and discretion."[11]

The great and fundamental difference between entering a theological school to study to be a pastor and entering a law school, or a medical school, or an engineering school must be maintained. This means respect for the ways in which the Holy Spirit works usually through the ordinary means of grace in the community of faith, while at the same time remembering that God chooses when and where he pleases.

The ordinary means of grace were, in the Presbyterian Church U.S., the communal context out of which young people were called into the ministry as late as the 1950s. The first context was the Christian home. The second context was the worship of the congregation. The third was youth work in churches, conferences, and quadrennial conventions that concentrated on teaching the faith and the church's mission to proclaim the gospel. Ministries on college campuses flourished in the 1950s with a great emphasis on Bible study. Youth work, conferences, and campus ministries all began a precipitous decline in the 1960s. Insofar as they continued, the emphasis was increasingly on teaching about sex, race, or economic life, not the study of the Bible or teaching the faith.

Church colleges also moved away from their earlier commitments to teach the Old Testament and the New Testament, to teach the faith, and to nurture students in their Christian calling.

In 1982 Professor Jack R. Presseau of Presbyterian College, Clinton, South Carolina, published an article in the *Presbyterian Outlook* calling attention to the radical decline of candidates for the ministry on Presbyterian church college campuses who intended to go to Presbyterian seminaries. No one seemed to take the article seriously, though some colleagues in college and church work were offended that he said publicly what was clearly documentable and ominous for the future of the church.[12]

In the recruitment of students the church and seminary interact. The breakup of the old context of youth programs designed to teach the faith, of campus ministries that emphasized Bible study as well as teaching the faith, of church colleges that gave students the opportunity to engage in the academic enterprise in the context of a Christian interpretative framework and Christian worship deprived the seminary and church of the context in which ministers of the Word are called. The consequences of this breakdown is most clear in the decline in young white males entering the ministry.

The old context for the calling of ministers appears to survive today primarily in evangelical churches and colleges and in para-church groups. Without this old context for the calling of ministers, without what one former recruitment staff member calls the infrastructure, then the seminary's recruitment tends to become marketing.[13]

The church and the seminary have not faced the real problem. Instead the seminaries have sought students in other ways. One answer has been new programs, especially the Doctor of Ministry degree. Another has been an appeal to second-career persons. Yet second-career invitations to ministry are hazardous, especially when they are answered after failures in a first career and after a personal tragedy such as a divorce. Still another answer is the advocacy of Commissioned Lay Pastors, a program that, if enacted, will have a dramatic impact on seminary and church alike.

The Call Today

The recovery of the structures, the communities and especially the awareness of the holy, the context in which persons were called to the ministry, will not come easily or quickly for old-line churches. In the context of what remains of the ordinary means of grace we can in the recruitment of ministers insist on at least five directives:

1. The call to the ministry that the church makes must emphasize the prior call of God. The ministry is not a job but a calling. It is not simply a way of making a living. It is a calling that requires commitment and sacrifice.

In calling its ministers, the church in all its appeals must act and speak in the language of the New Testament and in the context of the worshiping, teaching, obeying church. The call begins in the depths of the church's life. It comes in the teaching, nurturing of children, in the fellowship of youth activities in which young people not only learn the Bible narratives and language of faith, the theology of the church but also the joy of Christian fellowship and service. God calls a person when and where he chooses, but the call is not likely to come outside the church, outside authentic Christian community.

Any admissions program of a seminary must presuppose this long history of life in the church. Otherwise the seminary's program may become marketing. A large seminary student body may mean trouble for the church. A small student body who have been truly called may be a great asset.

2. Seminaries in recruiting students for the ministry have a second responsibility, namely, to be honest about the *limits* and *possibilities* of pastorates. This honesty begins with the recognition that two-thirds

of the Presbyterian churches in the Presbyterian Church (U.S.A.)
have 199 or fewer members and three-fourths have 299 or fewer
members. Moreover, the work of the pastorate overwhelmingly is
the pastoral care of ordinary people dealing with the ordinary trials of
life. It is also teaching the faith to congregations made up of busy people who are inundated by television and other secular distractions.
Many of the personal rewards of being the pastor of a church come
after a long time. Seminary students should not be under any illusions
about the glamour or the excitement of a pastorate.

Increasingly seminary students seek to go to staffs of large churches
and then from those staffs to sizable congregations. This is a more ex-
citing introduction to the ministry, but participation on the staff of a
large church does not teach the reality of church life as being the pastor of a small congregation does.

Seminaries in some way must instill into students a great confidence that the preaching of the Word of God is never without consequences, but at the same time they must prepare students for the
discouragements that are inevitable in a pastorate, especially in the
short run. The great blessings of being a pastor frequently come only
after many years.

The seminary in helping the students to see the reality of the pastorate must also give them a vision of what is possible by the power
of the Holy Spirit. Robert E. Speer, Secretary of the Presbyterian
Board of Foreign Missions (1891–1937) and church statesman, once
said that the great time for missions is when any person has a gospel
to proclaim. The same is true in the pastorate. The great time in the
pastorate is when the preacher has the gospel to proclaim, a faith to
teach, and in the light of this faith and teaching a ministry of healing
and support in pastoral care.

Seminaries must respect the limits of what any seminary or church
organization can do either in the calling of a minister or in the support of a minister in a pastorate. Yet within these limits the seminary
ought to always keep open for students the *indeterminate possibilities* of
a pastorate for the service of God.

3. The call to the ministry includes the dimension of sacrifice. This
call to sacrifice should be clearly articulated in the recruitment of
seminary students, just as it is clearly enunciated throughout the New
Testament. Yet the meaning of sacrifice is difficult to communicate
today; for the church, like society, has affluent pastors, executives,

seminary professors, and administrators whose affluence could not have been imagined as late as the early 1970s. Like society at large, we also have churches the vast majority of which have few members and little financial resources. It was easier for seminary graduates to know this when I attended the seminary in 1940. By present standards life at Columbia Seminary was below the poverty level for faculty and students alike. When I became a professor at Union Theological Seminary, James Jones, the president, insisted that teaching at Union was different from teaching at the University of Virginia. Professors were expected to make sacrifices and to do extra work in the church without honoraria for the sake of the call. This is now a forgotten message. I know ministers who today out of a great sense of call are living sacrificially to do their work. On the other hand, for many the ministry now involves no sacrifice. I do not know specifically how the sense of sacrifice can be incorporated again in the call, in the most affluent society in human history and in an affluent denomination. In any case we must avoid sentimentalizing sacrifice or, worse still, corrupting it as when some have claimed giving up their weekends on the lake was a great sacrifice. Yet much work in the church will have to be done by people who genuinely live sacrificially, or it will not be done. The great challenge in recruitment today is to call people to be *servants* of Jesus Christ in the work of the church.

4. In recruiting students, seminaries must be realistic, not only about the church but also about the abilities necessary for an effective pastor. The minister of a church must be an administrator, an organizer, a leader and initiator of actions, as well as a preacher, teacher, and pastor. Many persons, who can be effective in many fields of work, including teaching in a seminary, do not have the range of abilities to be effective pastors. In addition an effective pastor must be a person with the personal and physical capacities for hard work.

Seminaries, insofar as I can observe, recruit students without much consideration of the applicant's ability to gather a congregation, bring members into it, or raise a budget. This is unfair to the church and also to the students. Moreover, academic work in seminaries is not, so far as I can observe, very demanding. In fact it is difficult to fail a course in a seminary. On the basis of many years of teaching, it is my judgment that every student ought to enter a course knowing that failing the course is a possibility. Yet every professor soon learns that failing a student means time and trouble. Passing a student who does not qualify postpones the trouble for the church. If the ministry is a serious work, the education for the ministry must be as serious as a first-rate medical school or law school. Easy grading makes life on the campus pleasant but, as I have observed, leads to mediocrity if not disaster in the pastorate.

The high point in the education of a seminarian for the pastorate fifty years ago at Columbia Theological Seminary was student preaching. Each student was required to preach before the entire student body and faculty and then submit to public criticism by the homiletics professor and briefer criticisms by all of the faculty in the presence of the student body. At Union Theological Seminary in Virginia in 1960 members of the senior class preached before the faculty and student body and then were subjected to public criticism in detail by two professors and in brief comment by other professors in the presence of the entire student body. In my own experience I have never preached three better prepared sermons than those I preached before the faculty and student body at Columbia Theological Seminary. In the mid-1960s student preaching was eliminated from the requirements at Union Theological Seminary on the grounds that this public evaluation of sermons was harmful to the personalities of the young students. I had just come from a pastorate in a university community where football players, some of whom worshiped in the church of which I was pastor, had to perform before the cheers and also the jeers of tens of thousands of people every Saturday. More than that, they were subject to strict grading on the part of their coaches. These grades were public knowledge, sometimes being published in the newspapers.

I never understood why theological students preparing for the arduous task of leadership in a local congregation should have more tender personalities than football players. I often wished that more candidates for the ministry took their preparation for the ministry as seriously as athletes took their preparation to play football or to engage in the Olympics.

5. The call of the seminary and the church must be sharply focused. The church's ministers are not called to do good in general, but to be ministers of the Word of God. They are to preach the gospel, administer the sacraments, and exercise pastoral care. They are to go out in the byways and hedges and invite people into the context of the means of grace, to accept Jesus Christ as Savior and Lord.

The Renewal of the Church
as a Community of Grace and Nature

The conclusion of the matter is that the call to the ministry is first of all God's call and beyond our comprehending. Our human activities, as important as they are, are secondary to God's call. This much is clear. Our human activities must presuppose life in the worshiping, believing community. Otherwise, recruitment for the ministry becomes *marketing*, scarcely distinguishable from recruitment for General Electric or McDonald's, with disastrous consequences for the church.

The recovery or repair of the communal context of the intentional means of grace out of which persons have been traditionally called to be ministers of the Word of God will likely take time. It cannot be accomplished by a committee action or the direction of a governing body. Communities grow out of life. The context out of which ministers are most likely to be called will come only with the renewal of the congregations as a worshiping, believing people. In calling ministers the church must do the best it can with what now exists. Yet it must continually work and pray for the continual renewal of the community that claims the intentional means of grace and provides the context of preaching, teaching, nurture, and fellowship out of which persons are more likely to be called to be ministers of the Word.

Epilogue

The crisis in the seminary and in the church is easy to describe in quantifiable terms. The underlying causes of the crisis are harder to diagnose. A prescription for a recovery is most difficult of all.

Is there any hope that the seminary will contribute to a revival of the Presbyterian tradition and community in our time? Is there ground for believing that the Presbyterian manner of life and the Presbyterian understanding of Christian faith will once again strengthen, not only individual lives, but also communities, and in so doing contribute to the health of the broader community of American society?

I began by saying that I was born a Presbyterian and I cherish the tradition that has been bequeathed to me by those who have gone before. I believe on easily documentable grounds that this tradition has been a significant factor in building the society that we now enjoy in the United States of America, the greatest political and social achievement of the human race on this planet.

I also rejoice in the tradition that enabled people to live, sometimes in hard and always challenging circumstances, in the first several centuries of their existence in this country with the serenity, poise, and dignity that is wrested by faith in the living God from the raw stuff of life. I long that this tradition will once again become alive for increasing numbers of people in our society.

Signs of hope are appearing. The best sign of hope is the vitality of local congregations where the gospel is preached and pastoral care is exercised. In a declining denomination many local congregations in highly diverse communities and situations have more vitality and strength than they have ever had in their history. If the church can be renewed in local congregations, it can be renewed on a denominational level.

The simple fact is that wherever the gospel is preached, the churches today show signs of great and vigorous vitality. In addition there are signs that younger people in our society once again long to hear the gospel preached, and wish to bring up their children in the faith. I have experienced this over and over again in churches such as Peachtree Presbyterian Church in Atlanta, Georgia; First Presbyterian Church, Gastonia, North Carolina; First Presbyterian Church, Charlotte, North Carolina; White Memorial Presbyterian Church, Raleigh, North Carolina, and First Presbyterian Church, Wilmington, North Carolina.

We can hope that the signs of renewal that are found in many local congregations will soon appear on many seminary campuses. When seminary campuses recover a passion for preaching the gospel of what God has done in Jesus Christ for our salvation, the revival in the church will be well under way.

Committees and retreats, as I have indicated earlier in the book, do not show much promise for the renewal of either the church or the seminary. For one thing the committees are frequently made up of persons who have been advocates of failed policies and whose commitments lie at the heart of the problem. Tenured faculty and the staying power of bureaucratic appointments makes the possibilities of change very slow. Finally, any real change that shall dramatically transform either the seminary or the declining statistics in our church will have to come from renewal deep in personal and communal life. The vitalization of the church depends on people of deep faith and personal strength who have the *courage* to *stand* for their faith and not to be blown about by every wind of doctrine and every advocacy cause. The recovery of people of deep Christian faith and of personal strength, who are self-determining, who are able to put personal integrity ahead of career ambitions, may be taking place now. This is a cause for hope.

A further cause for hope is the evidence that American people are very open to the gospel. Perhaps never before in American history have so many people been reaching out for some word from the Lord. This should be a special ground for hope for Presbyterians. The first Reformed Christians in Switzerland were not so much concerned about a guilty conscience as they were about the question, Is there a word from the Lord? Is human existence the expression of purpose, intentionality, and love? Is there at the heart of things a God who is *personal* and who in Jesus Christ has *acted* for our salvation?

We were told in the early 1960s that modern people were no longer religious, that they no longer asked the religious questions. There is evidence that this is wrong. People still ask the old question of Parmenides, "Why is there something and not nothing?" They not only ask this question but they go on to ask, Why is there life rather than a lifeless world; why is there personal life and not impersonal existence; why does the human spirit have the power to transcend every human achievement and ask for something more? These were the questions asked sixteen centuries ago by Augustine. Today we are the beneficiaries of the answers of Christian faith that he formulated.

Reformed theology placed its emphasis on a personal God who acts personally in the created orders of nature and history and who has made himself known in many diverse ways but especially in Jesus Christ, who is God incarnate, and on the Bible as the written Word of God. Some can no longer affirm this faith, but for those who do, the fields are white unto the harvest. Jesus Christ is the answer to the question God has placed deep within the human soul. The plight of the church today was well expressed in the words of John Milton, "The hungry sheep look up, and are not fed" (*Lycidas*).

In seminaries and in the leadership of church we have to learn once again that people do not go to church to hear about politics or about the feminist movement or about the black caucus or about conflict management. They come to hear about what God has done for human beings and for their salvation, to hear the Christian hope in the presence of death.

Hope has still a deeper foundation. God made the world, as Augustine so powerfully declares, so that evil cannot sustain itself. Evil is always parasitic on the good and more than this it always self-destructs. The same can be said of bad theology in the church and in a culture informed by Christian faith. Bad theology, that is theology that evacuates the content of the New Testament witness and the classic Christian affirmations, lives off of good theology. Bad theology on university and seminary campuses can attract students only because of worshiping congregations who do believe the gospel of what God has done in Jesus Christ. Theology that evacuates the strong content of Christian faith cannot gather or build churches and, it should be added, seminaries. It cannot sustain itself.

The recovery of faith and the achievement of a mature human life formed by the faith and capable of *self-determination* cannot be programmed. Faith and human greatness always come as gifts. We cannot program them and we cannot guarantee them, but there is the promise that if we gather together in the name of God, God shall be there. We have the hope that as we participate in worship and as we fellowship in the context of the appointed means of grace we may receive that which we cannot program. This will be the foundation for the renewal of the seminaries and the church.

There are, however, two concrete suggestions with which I would like to close this book.

The first is the word of Jesus: "Let your word be 'Yes, Yes' or 'No, No'; anything more than this comes from the evil one" (Matthew 5:37).

Seminary administrations and trustees must learn that the problems of a theological seminary cannot be solved by public relations or slick paper publications. Every seminary I know is spending a huge sum of money on public relations. In many cases seminary publications are propaganda. A seminary publication, above all others, should be scrupulously honest and open. Anything less than this can only lead to deeper trouble. Seminary public relations are most effective when what they say corresponds to what actually is.

Seminary administrations must also learn that there is no substitute for openness and accountability in the use of money and in particular in the use of endowments. The very fact that the church does not have a large free press such as keeps the civil society under surveillance means that seminaries as well as administrations generally should take the leading responsibility in making all of their records open to the public. It is a tragic situation when citizens of the commonwealth have better access to what is going on at a state university than they do to what is actually going on at a seminary campus.

This admonition of Jesus is also directed to theologians. Theologies that would have no appeal to people, if they were truly understood, are covered up with Christian rhetoric and words so that the ordinary reader does not understand what the theologian is actually saying. The theologian above all others should let his or her "yea" be "yea" and "nay" be "nay." In any case a theology that neglects the classic doctrines of Christian faith ought not to be covered up with a Christian rhetoric that deceives the ordinary reader. The renewal of life on seminary campuses will begin when we let our yeses be yes and our noes be no and when what we say to the people in local congregations is an honest report of what we are actually saying and doing on seminary campuses.

The second crucial word, as I indicated earlier, is the question Jesus put to his disciples, "But who do you say that I am?" (Matthew 16:15). The answer to this question is as crucial to us as it was to the disciples. Who do we say that Jesus Christ is? In an Enlightenment society there are great pressures to say that he was a stoic wise man, a prophet, or a teacher. There is always the continual pressure in a pluralistic society to say that, even if he is the Word of God made flesh, he is only one of many words. This pressure exists in every civic club I know and in some religion (no longer Bible) departments on church college campuses. The pressure exists alas on seminary campuses.

As I have observed the church, both as a seminary professor and as a minister, I am increasingly convinced that our inability to give a clear New Testament answer to this question is at the heart of the crisis in the church. On every page, the New Testament attempts to say that in Jesus Christ God acted for our salvation. John puts it very clearly, Jesus Christ is the Word, the mind of God, God in God's self-expression, embodied in a human life. The apostle Paul in a letter to the Colossians declares, "He is the image of the invisible God, the firstborn of all creation; for in him all things in heaven and on earth were created, things visible and invisible, whether thrones or dominions or rulers or powers—all things have been created through him and for him. He himself is before all things, and in him all things hold together" (Colossians 1:15–17).

The writer of Hebrews declares, "Long ago God spoke to our ancestors in many and various ways by the prophets, but in these last days he has spoken to us by a Son, whom he appointed heir of all things, through whom he also created the worlds. He is the reflection of God's glory and the exact imprint of God's very being, and he sustains all things by his powerful word" (Hebrews 1:1–3).

The church lives by the passionate conviction that Jesus Christ is the embodiment of the wisdom and power of God, that in and through him God wrought our salvation and that when wicked people crucified him, God raised him from the dead. Without this passionate conviction, there is really no reason for the seminaries to exist. If Jesus Christ is not the Word made flesh and if God did not in truth, raise him from the dead, then we ought to return the endowments, close our seminaries, and do something more useful.

The crucial question that has to be put both to the church and to the seminary today is, Who do you say that I am? False answers will continue to empty churches.

Notes

Introduction

1. Alfred North Whitehead, *Adventures of Ideas* (New York: New American Library, 1955), 99.
2. See Ernest Trice Thompson, *Presbyterians in the South,* vol. 3: *1890–1972* (Richmond: John Knox Press, 1973), 410.
3. Cf. John H. Leith, *From Generation to Generation* (Louisville, Ky.: Westminster/John Knox Press, 1990), chap. 6. Statistical data are from *Minutes of the General Assembly of the Presbyterian Church (U.S.A.),* from *Mission Update* 18A: 1 (February 1989) and 22: 3 (July–September 1993); and from People in Mutual Mission, Louisville, Kentucky 1995.
4. 1960 data are from seminary catalogs; 1996 data are from current registrar announcements.
5. H. Richard Niebuhr, "Faith in Gods and God," in *Radical Monotheism and Western Culture* (New York: Harper & Brothers, 1960), 99.

Chapter 1.
The Crisis

1. Jeffrey K. Hadden, *The Gathering Storm in the Churches* (Garden City, N.Y.: Doubleday & Co. 1969), 3–33.
2. For confirmation of Charles Hodge's influence, see Mark Noll, *"The Princeton Review," Westminster Theological Journal* 50:2 (fall, 1988): 283–304; Peter Wallace and Mark Noll, "Students of Princeton Seminary, 1812–1929: A Research Note," *American Presbyterians* 72:3 (fall 1994): 203–15; Mark Noll, ed. *The Princeton Theology 1812–1921* (Grand Rapids: Baker Book House, 1983).
3. Eugene D. Genovese, *The Southern Front: History and Politics in the Cultural War* (Columbia, S.C.: University of South Carolina Press, 1992), 2–18, 167–77.
4. David S. Wells, ed., *Reformed Theology in America: A History of Its Modern Developments* (Grand Rapids: Wm. B. Eerdmans Publishing Co., 1986).
5. Among the presses publishing these books are Banner of Truth, Reformed Academic Press, Sprinkle Publications, Still Water Revival

Books, Preservation Press Books, Soli Deo Gloria, and Presbyterian and Reformed Publishing Co.

6. Philip Hammond, *Religion and Personal Autonomy: The Third Disestablishment in America* (Columbia, S.C.: University of South Carolina Press, 1992), 2–18, 167–77.

7. George Buttrick, "The Minister's Search for Self-Identity," May 12, 1974. Sermon tape in the Union Theological Seminary in Virginia library.

8. Jon D. Levenson, *The Hebrew Bible, the Old Testament, and Historical Criticism: Jews and Christians in Biblical Studies* (Louisville, Ky.: Westminster/John Knox Press, 1993), 117, 110, 125.

9. Jon Levenson, "Theological Liberalism Aborting Itself," *Christian Century* (February 5–12, 1992): 146.

10. Geoffrey Wainwright, "Seminaries in Crisis," *Challenge to Evangelism Today* (spring 1992) (Ed Robb Evangelistic Association): 5.

11. See Gilbert Meilaender's review of William Placher's *Narratives of a Vulnerable God* in *First Things* 56 (October 1995): 47.

12. Mary Midgley, *Women's Choices, Philosophical Problems Facing Feminism* (New York: St. Martin's Press, 1983), Esp. chap. 6.

13. See Kenneth Woodward, "Gender and Religion," *Commonweal* 113:10 (November 22, 1996): 9–14.

14. Aubrey Brown presented his case against presbyteries as ministerial unions very forcefully at the annual Union Theological Seminary in Virginia alumni/alumnae meeting in 1982.

Chapter 2.
The Boundaries of Christian Faith

1. G.W.H. Lampe, *God as Spirit* (London: Clarendon Press, 1977). Cf. R.P.C. Hanson, *The Continuity of Christian Doctrine* (New York: Seabury Press, 1981), 44.

2. Cf. François Wendel, *Calvin, the Origins and Development of His Religious Thought* (London: William Collins Sons & Co., 1963), 82–83.

3. A. A. Hodge, *A Commentary on the Confession of Faith* (Philadelphia: Presbyterian Board of Publications and Sabbath School Work, 1869), 542.

4. James D. G. Dunn, *Christology in the Making,* 2d ed. (London: SCM Press, 1992), 251–68.

5. Paul Tillich, *A History of Christian Thought* (New York: Simon & Schuster, 1968), 71–72.

6. See Stephen Sykes, *The Identity of Christianity* (Philadelphia: Fortress Press, 1984).

7. See Dean Kelley, *Why Conservative Churches Are Growing* (New York: Harper & Row, 1972); Thomas C. Reeves, *The Empty Church: The Sui-*

cide of Liberal Christianity (New York: Free Press, 1996); Les Parrott III and Robin D. Perrin, "The New Denominations," *Christianity Today* (March 11, 1991).

8. See Rosemary Ruether, *Sexism and God Talk* (Boston: Beacon Press, 1983).

9. John Calvin, *Reply to Sadolet,* in *Calvin: Theological Treatises,* Library of Christian Classics, vol. xxii (Philadelphia: Westminster Press, 1954), 228.

10. Panentheism cannot be justified in Reformed theology by an appeal to Zwingli according to recent interpreters. See W. P. Stephens, *The Theology of Huldrych Zwingli* (Oxford: Clarendon Press, 1986), 86; Gottfried W. Locher, *Zwingli's Thought, New Perspectives* (Leiden: E. J. Brill, 1981), 67, 123–24.

11. Cf. Gerhard Sauter, *The Question of Meaning* (Grand Rapids: Wm. B. Eerdmans Publishing Co., 1995).

12. Bertrand Russell, "A Free Man's Worship," in the *Basic Writings of Bertrand Russell* (London: George Allen & Unwin, 1961), 66ff.

13. I am indebted to Ian Barbour for the theological significance of praying for rain. H. R. Mackintosh, in his critique of Schleiermacher, states that a person's real standpoint in theology is revealed unerringly in his view of prayer. *Types of Modern Theology* (London: Nisbet, 1942), 92.

14. Cf. John Polkinghorne, *The Faith of a Physicist* (Princeton, N.J.: Princeton University Press, 1994). In his Gifford Lectures 1993-1994, Polkinghorne, a distinguished theoretical physicist, affirms the agency of the personal God in creation. Over against panentheism and process theologies Polkinghorne affirmed "a personal God, able to react in particular ways to particular occurrences" (82). Polkinghorne wanted to affirm a God "who raised Jesus from the dead," adequate for "the remarkable phenomenon of hope; our account of divine agency will have to be adequate both to the fact of evil and to the fact of hope" (ibid).

Again he writes, "I do not want to be just a fly stuck in the amber of divine remembrance. I look forward to a destiny and a continuing life beyond death. To put it bluntly, the God of process theology does not seem to be the God who raised Jesus from the dead" (68).

15. John Macquarrie, "Some Thoughts on Heresy," *Christianity and Crisis* 26:22 (December 26, 1966): 291–94.

16. Benton Johnson, Dean R. Hoge, Donald A. Luidens, "Mainline Churches: The Real Reason for Decline," *First Things* 31 (March 1993): 13ff.

17. Jon Levenson, "Theological Liberalism Aborting Itself," *Christian Century* (February 5–12, 1992): 139.

18. Thomas Oden, "Can We Talk about Heresy?" *Christian Century* (April 12, 1995): 390.

19. Karl Barth, *Church Dogmatics*, I/1, rev. ed., trans. G. W. Bromiley (Edinburgh: T. & T. Clark, 1975), 26ff.

20. Ibid., 87.

21. Ibid., 82f.

22. Barth, *Church Dogmatics* IV/3.1 (1961), §69, sec. 2; also IV/3.2 (1962), §71, sec. 4.

23. H.E.W. Turner, *The Pattern of Christian Truth* (London: A. R. Mowbray & Co., 1954), 101–2.

24. Thomas Oden and Leicester Longden, eds., *Collected Essays of Albert C. Outler* (Grand Rapids: Zondervan Publishing House, 1991), 40 ff.

25. Ibid., 43.

26. H.E.W. Turner, *Pattern of Christian Truth*, 498.

27. Julian N. Hartt, *A Christian Critique of American Culture* (New York: Harper & Row, 1967), 131, 322, 346.

Chapter 3.
Teaching the Church's Faith

1. James Turner, *Without God, Without Creed* (Baltimore: Johns Hopkins University Press, 1985), 266–67.

2. Many of these summaries, such as Francis Turretin's *Institutes of Elenctic Theology,* contain detailed theological analysis. The scholastic theologians, building on past achievements, knew the theological nuances and issues, saving the theologians who came after them much work. For this reason contemporary theologians, whose own commitments are far to the left of Turretin, find his work very useful. For the same reason A. A. Hodge's *Outlines of Theology* is very useful for any young minister.

3. Some theologians such as Karl Rahner have written brilliant theologies in nonbiblical language, but to my knowledge they have not been influential beyond academic communities.

4. William Haller, *The Rise of Puritanism* (New York: Harper & Brothers, 1938), 128ff.

5. Robert Morgan and John Burton, *Biblical Interpretation* (New York: Oxford University Press, 1988), 136–37.

6. George Lindbeck, "Scripture Consensus and Community," *This World Journal of Religion and Public Life* (fall 1988): 11–12.

7. Jon D. Levenson, *The Hebrew Bible, the Old Testament, and Historical Criticism: Jews and Christians in Biblical Studies* (Louisville, Ky.: Westminster/John Knox Press, 1993), 117–25 (p. 119; the words are quoted from Leo Strauss, *Natural Right and History* [Chicago and London: University of Chicago Press, 1950], 25).

8. For a critique of the Jesus Seminar, see Luke Timothy Johnson, *The Real Jesus, The Misguided Quest for the Historical Jesus and the Truth of the*

Traditional Gospels (San Francisco: Harper, 1996); N. T. Wright, *Who Was Jesus?* (Grand Rapids: Wm. B. Eerdmans Publishing Co., 1992); Richard Hays, "The Corrected Jesus," *First Things* (1994): 43–48 (43).

9. Christopher Seitz, "Pluralism and the Lost Art of Apology," *First Things* (June–July 1994): 15–18.

10. Ernst Benz emphasized this observation in a lecture given in August of 1951 at the Ecumenical Institute held at Woudschoten, the Netherlands. This observation did not impress me at the time as it does today. Theologians should be honest and should not write and speak in a manner that deceives believers.

11. E. L. Mascall, *Jesus, Who He Is and How We Know Him* (London: Darton, Longman & Todd, 1985), 19.

12. Ernest L. Boyer, *Scholarship Reconsidered, Priorities of the Professoriate* (Princeton, N.J.: The Carnegie Foundation for the Advancement of Teaching, 1990), 9.

13. See Bradley J. Longfield "For God, for Country, and for Yale: Yale, Religion and Higher Education," in George M. Marsden and Bradley J. Longfield, *The Secularization of the Academy* (New York: Oxford University Press, 1992), 146–69.

Chapter 4.
Teaching Church Practice

1. Jean-Daniel Benoit, *Calvin directeur d'âmes* (Strasbourg, 1947).

2. Amy Nelson Burnett, *The Yoke of Christ: Martin Bucer and Christian Discipline,* Sixteenth Century Essays and Studies, 27 (Kirksville, Mo.: *Sixteenth Century Journal Publishers,* 1994), esp. chaps. 3 and 4.

3. *The Common Places of Martin Bucer,* trans. and ed. David Wright (Appleford, England: Sutton Courtenay Press, 1972), 21.

4. Richard Baxter, *The Reformed Pastor* (London: SCM Press, 1956), 48.

5. See Don S. Browning, *A Fundamental Practical Theology* (Minneapolis: Fortress Press, 1991), especially his discussion of the theology of Reinhold Niebuhr as including practical reason in serious theological and ethical discussions.

6. Seward Hiltner, *Preface to Pastoral Care* (Nashville: Abingdon Press, 1958).

7. Thomas Oden, *Care of Souls in the Classic Tradition* (Philadelphia: Fortress Press, 1989).

8. Eduard Thurneysen, *A Theology of Pastoral Care* (Richmond: John Knox Press, 1962), chap. 3.

9. Karl Barth, *Church Dogmatics* IV/3.2, p. 886.

10. This is a problem not only for the seminary but also for other fields. See Elizabeth A. Gowdy, "From Technical Rationality to Participating Consciousness," *Social Work* 39:4 (July 1994): 362–70.

Chapter 5.
On Choosing a Seminary Professor

1. According to an unpublished report of the Special Committee on Theological Education to the 1990 General Assembly, Presbyterian seminary faculty received *terminal* degrees as follows: University of Chicago 18, Harvard 17, Yale 16, Union Theological Seminary, New York City 14, Princeton Theological Seminary 10, Columbia University 9, Swiss universities (Basel and Zurich) 9, Duke 8, Vanderbilt 8, University of Edinburgh 6.
2. Ernest L. Boyer, *Scholarship Reconsidered, Priorities of the Professoriate* (Princeton, N.J.: The Carnegie Foundation for the Advancement of Teaching, 1990), 15.
3. Ibid., 17ff.
4. Ibid., 27.
5. Cf. Anne Matthews, *Bright College Years: Inside the American Campus Today* (New York: Simon & Schuster, 1997). This study of the college campus throws light on what is happening on seminary campuses.

Chapter 6.
The Moral Use of Endowments

1. Data provided by Presbyterian Church (U.S.A.) Foundation.
2. Merle Curti and Roderick Nash, *Philanthropy in the Shaping of American Higher Education* (New Brunswick, N.J.: Rutgers University Press, 1965), 5–6.
3. Ibid., 13–17.
4. Ibid., 17–18.
5. Robert Kingdon, "Calvin and the Government of Geneva" in *Calvinus Ecclesiae Genevensis Custos,* ed. Wilhelm Neuser (New York: Peter Lang, 1984), 51.
6. Jenny Wormald, *Court, Kirk, and Community: Scotland 1470–1625* (Toronto: University of Toronto Press, 1981), 76, 88.
7. Donald G. Miller, *The Scent of Eternity: A Life of Harris Elliott Kirk of Baltimore* (Macon, Ga.: Mercer University Press, 1989), 325ff.
8. Ibid., 326ff.
9. Based on correspondence with Robert J. Powell, Jr., a McNair descendant, of Washington, North Carolina.
10. Ernest Trice Thompson, *Presbyterians in the South,* vol. 3: *1890–1972* (Richmond: John Knox Press, 1973), 313–14.
11. Ibid., 329–30.
12. *Vantage,* spring 1990.
13. Based on my memory of conversations with F. Sydney Anderson, Jr., for-

mer business manager of Columbia Theological Seminary (1962–1987), who reported conversations with Dr. Richards in which Richards expressed concern that Columbia Seminary was not as faithful to the Westminster Confession as the trust required. F. Sydney Anderson Jr. confirmed my memory of these conversations in a letter dated August 31, 1996.

14. The Speer and Luce Libraries at Princeton Theological Seminary are located on land given by James Lenox with the specification that if the seminary departed from the doctrines of the Confession and Catechisms the grant was null and void (William K. Selden, *Princeton Theological Seminary, a Narrative History 1812–1992* [Princeton University Press, 1992], 39, 57–65).

Robert L. and Alexander Stuart also gave real estate to the seminary on which buildings now stand with the provision that if the doctrines of the Confession as they were then understood should cease to be taught the land should revert to the Stuarts and their heirs.

The large part of the real estate of the Seminary, given by James Lenox and Robert L. and Alexander Stuart, is guarded from perversion by stringent conditions and doctrinal definitions. In the case of the gift of the Stuarts the deed provides as follows:

"Provided always, nevertheless, and upon condition that, if at any time or times, hereafter, the said parties of the second part, or their successors, shall pass from under the supervision and control of the General Assembly of the Presbyterian Church, in the United States of America, and its successors; and if at any time or times the leading doctrines declared by the Confession of Faith and Catechism of the Presbyterian Church, such as the doctrine of Universal and Total Depravity, the doctrine of Election, the doctrine of the Atonement, the doctrine of the Imputation of Adam's sin to all his posterity, and of the Imputation of Christ's righteousness to all His people for their justification, the doctrine of Human Inability and the doctrine of the Necessity of the Influence of the Holy Spirit in the regeneration, conversion and sanctification of sinners, as these doctrines are now understood and explained by the aforesaid General Assembly, shall cease to be taught and inculcated in the said Seminary, then, and in either of such cases, the grant and conveyance hereby made shall cease, and become null and void, and the said premises shall therefore revert to the said Robert L. Stuart and Alexander Stuart, their heirs and assigns, as in their first and former estate." ("Princeton Seminary," *Encyclopedia of the Presbyterian Church in the United States of America,* ed. Alfred Nevin [Philadelphia: Presbyterian Encyclopedia Publishing Co., 1884].)

The generosity and the faith of Christian believers such as Lenox, the

Stuarts, and William Green in the nineteenth century made possible the Princeton of today. The only proper response to this faith and generosity of the founders of our seminaries is gratitude and humility combined with a moral commitment to respect and honor their trusts.

Chapter 7.
Seminary Constituencies and Boards

1. Proceedings of the General Assembly of the Presbyterian Church (U.S.A.), in *Minutes of the 208th General Assembly (1986)*, Part I: *Journal*, 53ff.
2. Ibid.
3. Peter F. Drucker, "The Age of Social Transformation," *Atlantic Monthly* (November 1994): 53–80.
4. Two names stand out in my memory: John Watlington, elder in First Presbyterian Church, Winston-Salem, North Carolina, and president of Wachovia Bank, and Charles Myers, elder in First Presbyterian Church, Greensboro, North Carolina, and president of Burlington Industries.
5. The critiques I have made of seminary boards are very similar to the critiques of boards of nonprofit organizations made by Thomas Holland in his book *Improving the Performance of Governing Boards* (Phoenix: Oryx Press, 1996).

   See also *Renewing the Academy Presidency, Stronger Leadership for Tougher Times,* Report of the Commission on the Academic Presidency (Washington, D.C.: Association of Governing Boards of Universities and Colleges, 1996). The report includes the following comment concerning trustees: "Unfortunately, too many trustees lack a basic understanding of higher education or significant commitment to it" (11). This report, written primarily for colleges and universities, is applicable to seminaries.

Chapter 8.
The Recruitment of Students

1. Ellis L. Larsen and James M. Shropshire, "A Profile of Contemporary Seminarians," *Theological Education* 24:2 (spring 1988).
2. Reinhold Niebuhr, *Leaves from the Notebook of a Tamed Cynic* (New York: Da Capo Press, 1976), 64–65.
3. John B. Adger and John L. Girardeau, eds., *The Collected Writings of James Henley Thornwell* (Richmond: Presbyterian Committee of Publications, 1873), 4:24.
4. Ibid., 25.
5. John Calvin, *Calvin: Institutes of the Christian Religion,* ed. John T. McNeill; trans. Ford Lewis Battles (Philadelphia: Westminster Press, 1960).

6. Ibid.
7. *Collected Writings of James Henley Thornwell* 4:29.
8. Ibid., 27.
9. Ibid., 28–29.
10. Ibid., 30.
11. *Calvin: Institutes of the Christian Religion* 4.3.12.
12. Jack R. Presseau, "Pendulum Swings and Pre-Ministerial Preparation," *Presbyterian Outlook* (April 12, 1982): 13–14.
13. Roger A. Nicholson, formerly admissions direction at Union Theological Seminary in Virginia, has discussed these issues with me and I am grateful for his insights.